ST JAMES'S PALACE
A HISTORY

Kenneth Scott

SCALA

This edition © Scala Publishers Ltd 2010

Text © Kenneth Scott 2010

Reproductions of all items in the Royal Collection
© 2010 Her Majesty Queen Elizabeth II

First published in 2010 by
Scala Publishers Ltd
Northburgh House
10 Northburgh Street
London EC1V 0AT, UK
www.scalapublishers.com

ISBN: 978 1 85759 659 5

Text by Kenneth Scott
Edited by Sandra Pisano
Designed by hoopdesign.co.uk
Printed in China

10 9 8 7 6 5 4 3 2 1

Page 1: The State Apartments: the approach to the Throne Room from the Queen Anne Room; pp 2–3: *St James's Park and the Mall* (after 1745, attributed to Joseph Nickolls); page 5: The Throne in the State Apartments; page 6: The Grand Staircase by Christopher Wren leading to the State Apartments; page 8: View from the doorway at the top of the Grand Staircase, showing the Armoury, with the Tapestry Room and Queen Anne Room beyond; pp 10–11: The Tapestry Room; pp 12–13: The Armoury.

BUCKINGHAM PALACE

St James's Palace has always had a special place in my affection. I was born in Clarence House and spent my early childhood there, and my husband and I now have an apartment in the Palace itself. St James's has been home to seventeen generations of the Royal Family, and its past is linked to many of the great events in our history. Today other members of the Royal Family, as well as a few senior members of the Royal Household, also live in the Palace, but much of it is occupied by offices; it houses the headquarters of the Royal Collection, and is also home to The Queen's Guard and to The Queen's traditional bodyguards, the Gentlemen at Arms and the Yeomen of the Guard. The State Apartments are still in frequent use for receptions, dinners and meetings of charities and organisations with a royal connection.

This book tells the story of the development of the Palace from its first construction by King Henry VIII on the site of a hospital for leprous maidens to the additions made over the centuries by such famous architects as Inigo Jones, Sir Christopher Wren and John Nash; and gives an interesting account of some of the remarkable people who have lived there. Many of them are depicted in portraits, mostly from the Royal Collection, and the book is richly illustrated to show that behind the somewhat unassuming exterior of the Palace are a magnificent series of State Apartments which were once the principal seat of the monarchy – the "Court of St James's". I hope you enjoy reading this fascinating piece of history.

Anne

1

THE LEPER HOSPITAL

St James's Palace is the least well known of all royal residences. The great Clock Tower at the bottom of St James's Street – one of the oldest parts of the palace – is a familiar landmark, and every Londoner knows Clarence House, where for many years crowds gathered on the birthday of Queen Elizabeth the Queen Mother, and which is now the home of the Prince of Wales and his family. After the death of Diana Princess of Wales thousands of people congregated outside St James's to lay flowers against the walls, and queued to sign the Book of Condolence at the Chapel Royal, where her coffin rested before her funeral. But few members of the public have been inside the palace, unless they have been invited to attend one of the many receptions held in the State Apartments by charities associated with a member of the Royal Family, or to receive the Duke of Edinburgh's Gold Award. St James's is now never lived in by the Sovereign, despite the fact that formal State documents are often said to be 'Given at Our Court of St James's', and that foreign Ambassadors in London are traditionally accredited to the Court of St James's. Compared with Buckingham Palace, Windsor Castle and Hampton Court it is rather a modest building, looking more like an Oxford or Cambridge college than a palace. Yet although it is so little known, St James's Palace was once the principal royal residence in London, and it has a rich and colourful history which goes back more than 900 years.

The story begins with, of all things, a leper hospital – one of the first in the London area. Some time towards the end of the eleventh century a group of philanthropic citizens of London presented a piece of land to the parish of St Margaret's, Westminster, for the establishment of a hospital for 'fourteen leprous maiden sisters' who were to live there 'chastely and honestly in divine service'; the hospital was dedicated to Saint James the Less. Leprosy had been brought into England from the East by traders and pilgrims earlier in the eleventh century (one of the earliest recorded deaths from the disease was that of a Bishop of London in 1044) and it became, with the Black Death, one of the two major scourges of medieval England. It was believed to be highly contagious, and there was no known cure; lepers were therefore generally regarded with fear and revulsion, and they were ostracised and forbidden to move freely among their fellow citizens. The first two recorded leper hospitals were established in Kent before 1096; they later came to be known as 'lazar hospitals', from the belief that the Lazarus whom Christ raised from the dead had suffered from the disease. These hospitals offered no medical treatment to their inmates, but were merely places where those with the disease could be shut away from the rest of the population. During the reign of King Henry I (1100–35) lepers seem to have been regarded more charitably. His Queen, Matilda, was one of the first to treat those afflicted as human beings – she is said to have received them in her home (probably the Palace of Westminster) and to have washed and kissed them. She also founded London's second leper hospital, at St Giles in the Fields, to the north of Westminster.

But the majority of people regarded these unfortunates as social outcasts, and a papal decree of 1179, which was confirmed in 1200 by the Archbishop of Canterbury, ruled that lepers were not allowed to live with healthy men.

The site of St James's Hospital was doubtless therefore chosen because it was a long way from any other human habitation. It was a bleak spot in those days, on the edge of a low-lying, marshy stretch of land (now St James's Park) through which a branch of the River Tyburn flowed from the north to join the Thames near the little island of Thorney, where stood the Abbey and Palace of Westminster. To the north the land rose gently to a ridge of river gravel across which passed one of the main roads from the City of London to the west – roughly along the line of what is now Piccadilly – but there were probably no dwellings in the vicinity. No one knows exactly when the leper hospital was first built: John Stow in his *Survey of London* published in 1598 said that it had been established before the Norman Conquest, but the first record of its existence was in 1100 when it was visited by 'Giselbertus' (Gilbert Crispin), the Abbot of Westminster who had jurisdiction over it [1, 2].

The original grant of land to the hospital was 'two hides'. The 'hide' was, in the early Middle Ages, a variable measurement depending on whether the ground was cultivable; it was generally supposed to be the area of land adequate to support one family and its dependents. The two hides were probably not much less than the eventual holding of 160 acres recorded in 1531 (see page 24), including part of what

is now St James's Park and extending up the hill to what is now Piccadilly (traces of what may have been outbuildings of the hospital have been found in Arlington Street, just around the corner from the Ritz Hotel). In subsequent years the hospital received further charitable donations, both of land and of money. King Henry II, who reigned from 1154 to 1189, granted it a charter which guaranteed to the 'leprous maidens' their possessions, and encouraged people to give to them. A second charter by King John in 1205 again confirmed them in their possessions, which by this time included land in Hendon, Calcot (near

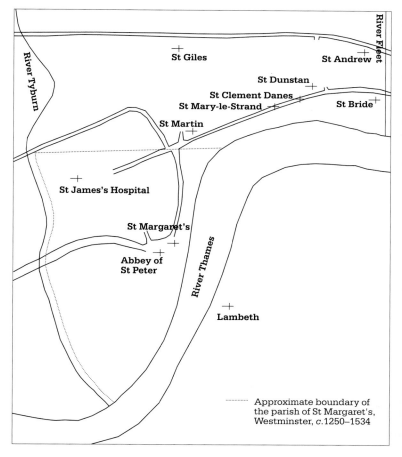

Approximate boundary of the parish of St Margaret's, Westminster, c.1250–1534

Reading) and in the City of London itself. Soon after this the hospital was rebuilt and enlarged, and eight brethren (of whom six were chaplains) were provided to minister to the sisters, with a Master appointed by the Abbot to supervise them. In 1209 King Edward I exempted the hospital from tax and granted to the brethren and sisters the privilege of holding a fair on the eve of St James's Day (25 July), and the following five days, as a means of augmenting their income. More lands were granted to the hospital in 1306 and a number of citizens of London made grants of money for its upkeep, but it never seems to have been a very rich foundation.

Meanwhile, in 1267, the hospital was provided with statutes laying down rules of behaviour for its inmates, and these were promulgated by the Papal Legate (Cardinal Ottobon) and the Abbot of Westminster (Richard de Ware). The number of inmates was increased to a maximum of 16 leprous virgins, one of whom was appointed Prioress by the Abbot, and eight brethren. One of the brethren was elected as Master and inducted by the Abbot. The inmates were to live by the rule of St Augustine, to say 60 'Aves' and 60 'Paternosters' a day, to make confession once a week and to receive communion four times a year. One tenth of the bread and meat in the house was to be distributed to leprous pilgrims and beggars; silence was to be observed at meals, which were limited to two a day; and there was to be no meeting between sisters and brethren except at meals and religious services. Anyone found guilty of 'incontinence' (i.e. sexual misconduct) was to receive corporal punishment.

To judge by the findings of successive visits by the Abbot, these rules were by no means strictly observed, and it is to be feared that the administration of the hospital left much to be desired. Following a visitation in 1277 the Abbot imposed a strict ban on fraternisation between sisters and brethren, and on excessive noise in the hospital. In 1317 the Master was accused of sequestering property and food from the sisters and brewing special beer for his own consumption, and one of the brethren was accused of frequent drunkenness and of misappropriating oblations offered to the hospital. Two years later it was found that some of the sisters had alienated hospital property in their wills, that sisters and brethren were dining together at all hours and that Holy Communion was not being celebrated even four times a year. By 1320 fields were uncultivated, houses in London belonging to the hospital were so derelict that tenants had to move out and the chapel roof had fallen in. By that time the number of residents had fallen to six sisters and three or four brethren, and the freedom with which they behaved would suggest that they may not all have been lepers – the incidence of the disease was in fact falling in England by this time, though it was not until the sixteenth century that it more or less died out.

The status of St James's Hospital as a refuge for the unfortunate, and a place of religious observance, finally came to an end in 1348, when the Black Death carried off all the remaining sisters and brethren except one, Walter de Weston, who ruled as Master over an empty house until he was removed three years later, after

19

which the hospital lay deserted for a time. By then a long-standing dispute about jurisdiction of the hospital between the King and the Abbot of Westminster had been resolved in favour of the Crown, and the post of Master of the Hospital seems to have become a sinecure granted by the King to a series of clerics who had duties elsewhere – they included a Dean of York, King Henry IV's physician, an Archdeacon of Sarum and a chaplain to King Henry VI. In 1379 one of the Masters, Thomas de Orgrave, was admonished for crenellating the tower of the hospital without licence (he claimed, naturally, that this was to improve security), and several years later he leased virtually all the hospital buildings to Lady Elizabeth de Despenser, the widow of a Knight of the Garter who had fought at the Battle of Poitiers. The Patent Roll recording this transaction gives us the only details we have of the hospital buildings, which had been renovated some 40 years before. The lease consisted of: *all the houses and buildings in the said Hospital within the gate of the long entrance before the door of the principal Hall, as well as the said Hall and Upper and Lower Chambers at each end of the Hall, and the stone tower as [well as] the Chamber above the said entrance, the Kitchen and Bakery and all other houses and buildings within the gate assigned for the Master's abode, with all the gardens, areas and stews* (i.e. fishponds) *within the said gate, excepting only a cellar newly constructed by the said Thomas for storing his wine.* No pictures of the hospital have survived and we can only imagine what the buildings looked like. The 'gate of the long entrance' is likely to have been to the north, leading towards the main road along the ridge, so it may

have been somewhere in what is now St James's Street. The 'principal Hall' may well have been on the site of the present Chapel Royal, with the other houses and buildings, including the 'stone tower', grouped around it. The hospital chapel, not mentioned in the lease, probably stood in what is now Colour Court, where recent excavations have uncovered the foundations and some human remains. The gardens probably extended to the east in the area now occupied by Marlborough House. It was clearly a substantial and comfortable residence for an elderly widow, and a far cry from the original modest refuge for 'fourteen leprous maidens'.

Lady Elizabeth was probably succeeded as tenant of the hospital buildings by others of whom we have no record, though it is likely that some of the Masters appointed by the King lived there themselves. We know that King Henry VI himself spent ten days there in March 1439 – the first royal resident – and in 1450 he granted perpetual custody of the hospital and its lands to Eton College, the school which he had founded in 1441 [3]. The incumbent Master, Thomas Kemp the King's Chaplain, was to be allowed to serve out his term, but he had by then been appointed Bishop of London and seems to have been content to resign the mastership, which from then on was held by the Provost of Eton. Kemp retained the principal building of the hospital, with the tower, as a tenant of Eton, but he lent it to his colleague the Bishop of Winchester who used it as his London residence. The Provost himself also seems to have used part of the hospital as a town *pied-a-terre*, and elsewhere in the

buildings there continued to live four alms-sisters and two chaplains, who were visited annually on St James's Day by the Provost and 30 of his young scholars.

In the Wars of the Roses Eton College supported the Lancastrian side, and when Henry VI was deposed in 1461 by the Yorkist, Edward IV, the College forfeited some of its possessions, including St James's Hospital, to the new king, who installed one of his clerks as Master. But in 1470 Henry VI returned to the throne and restored the hospital to Eton, in whose possession it remained until Henry VIII took it over in 1531 [4]. Four alms-sisters continued to live there, but the principal buildings were again leased out (at a rent of £5-6s–8d per annum) to secular tenants. These included Pietro Carmeliano (1451–1527) a poet, musician and scholar at the courts of Henry VII and Henry VIII who was described as 'Poet Laureate' when he edited a book published by Caxton in 1483. Another occupant of part of the hospital was Richard Grey, Earl of Kent (1481–1524), who was made a Knight of the Garter by Henry VII and was also a courtier of Henry VIII (he was present at the Field of the Cloth of Gold in 1520). He had inherited a 21-year lease of the 'great house' of the hospital from his father, to whom it had been granted in 1501 by the Provost of Eton. The alms-sisters themselves seem to have been ladies of substance: three of the last four who were pensioned off by Henry VIII were widows, and one of them, Dame Katherine Vampage, left a considerable amount of property in her will when she died. The Provosts of Eton thus appear to have begun the tradition of providing 'Grace and Favour' (i.e. rent free) accommodation at St James's, and the old leper hospital had become, in the words of one historian (Dr Gervase Rosser), 'a comfortable retirement home for the well-to-do'.

2

THE TUDOR PALACE

In October 1531 the Provost and Fellows of Eton College signed an indenture granting to King Henry VIII the hospital and lands of St James's in exchange for some pieces of land in Kent and Suffolk which were presumably surplus to the King's requirements [5]. The Provost cannot have been enthusiastic about losing St James's, which as we have seen had provided him with a convenient London base as well as a source of patronage and rental income. But in the previous five or six years a number of religious houses had been suppressed, and their assets confiscated, by Cardinal Wolsey to provide funds for the foundation of a new college at Oxford (now known as Christ Church); and following Wolsey's fall from favour in 1529, Thomas Cromwell, who had been his chief agent in this operation, had entered royal service and replaced his former master as the King's chief adviser and administrator. Cromwell had a reputation for ruthlessness, and it was clear that the King's subjects, however exalted, thwarted his wishes at their peril. Eton may well have considered itself fortunate to have been given something in exchange for the hospital.

The land which Henry acquired through this transaction (which was subsequently confirmed by Act of Parliament) included 64 acres to the south of 'the road between Charing Cross and Aye Hill' – probably roughly on the line of what is now Pall Mall – and 96 acres in the 'north fields' north of this road. These 160 acres were probably the 'two hides of land' which had been given to the hospital at its foundation in the eleventh century, and they represent nearly three times the area of the present St James's Park. In addition there were 25 acres further west, including some pieces of land in Knightsbridge, Chelsea and Fulham, and some scattered properties elsewhere in the London area which had been donated to the hospital by charitable benefactors over the years.

It is not clear why Henry decided to build a new palace on the site of the hospital. By 1531 he already had four palaces in London and Westminster, in addition to the Tower of London (which had become a fortress and prison rather than a palace, though it was customary for a new King to spend some nights there before his coronation). In 1512 the Royal Apartments in the old Palace of Westminster, which had until then been the principal royal residence in the capital, were largely destroyed by fire; but Henry had immediately set about building a new home, Bridewell Palace, on the south side of what is now the Strand, and it was virtually completed by 1525. Further east, near Blackfriars, was Baynards Castle, which had been rebuilt by Henry VII, who often stayed there, and which Henry VIII had given to his first queen, Catherine of Aragon. Finally, most splendid of all, there was Cardinal Wolsey's palatial residence of York Place (his official home as Archbishop of York) which he was in the process of rebuilding on a vast scale at the time of his downfall in 1529. The King took it over and called it 'the new Palace of Westminster', but it soon became known as Whitehall Palace and remained the Sovereign's principal London residence (replacing Bridewell) until it in turn was destroyed by fire at the end of the seventeenth century.

Detail of the fireplace in the
Tapestry Room, showing
the initials of Henry VIII
and Anne Boleyn with a
lovers' knot.

Outside London, building was going on at
Hampton Court (which the King had also
acquired from Wolsey) and at several of the
King's other country residences, including
Greenwich, Eltham and Nonsuch. Henry
had in fact embarked on a huge programme
of building and acquiring property, so
that by the end of his reign he owned
more than 60 residences – more than any
other Sovereign before or since – many of
which he had either built from scratch or
extensively refurbished.

With all this activity, why did the King
decide to build a fifth London palace at
St James's? His first objective in taking
over the hospital from Eton may well have
been to acquire the adjacent land, which
lay immediately to the west of his new
Whitehall 'leisure complex'. Shortly after
his deal with Eton College he also acquired
from the Abbot of Westminster, in exchange
for lands in Berkshire and elsewhere, a
further 80 acres to the south of the hospital.
He thus extended his holding of land to the
west of Whitehall Palace by a total of 144
acres south of Pall Mall, more than twice
the area of the present-day St James's Park,
and this would have extended at least as far
as the present site of Buckingham Palace.
He immediately enclosed and drained the
marshy land, and stocked it with game.
In 1533 he bought another six acres of
meadows near the hospital from a certain
Anthony Cotton, and in the same year one
of his Gentlemen Ushers, Thomas Alvard,
was appointed 'Keeper of the new Park
near Westminster'. There the King was
able to pursue his passion for hunting. The
hunting grounds extended far to the north
of the new park, and in 1546 Henry issued

Henry continued Wolsey's building
programme at Whitehall, adding not
only new Royal Apartments but also what
would now be called a 'leisure complex' to
the west of the palace (beyond the street
now called Whitehall) – three Real Tennis
courts, a tiltyard, a bowling alley and a
cockpit – for the diversion of himself and
his Court. At the same time more building
works were under way in the old Palace of
Westminster, which still housed the Law
Courts, the Exchequer and other offices.

a proclamation forbidding the hunting of hare, partridge, pheasant and heron by anyone other than himself in an area stretching from St James's Park to Islington, Highgate and Hampstead Heath.

Within this new estate lay the extensive buildings of St James's Hospital, and the King proceeded to pull them down and replace them. The idea of building a new palace there may have originated with Thomas Cromwell: when he entered the King's service he promised to make him 'the richest King that ever was in England', a promise which he later fulfilled by a number of profitable transactions, including the plundering of church funds and culminating in the Dissolution of the Monasteries [6]. The acquisition of St James's may well have been his first venture in the King's service: among his correspondence is a letter which he wrote in May 1530 to Wolsey from 'St James beside Westminster'. Since the hospital still belonged to Eton at that time, this suggests that Cromwell may have invited himself to stay there in order to assess its potential, and later brought it to the King's attention as a desirable property.

Henry obviously did not need a residence for himself so close to Whitehall. Some historians have suggested that St James's was intended as a home for Anne Boleyn, with whom the King was almost certainly having an affair by 1531, while the prolonged intrigues to bring about the annulment of his marriage to Catherine of Aragon were under way. In one of the oldest rooms in the palace (the Tapestry Room) there is a Tudor fireplace with the initials 'H A' and a lovers' knot, but this does not prove that Anne ever lived there: it was common practice for the initials of the King and Queen to be shown together in royal palaces, and the initials merely serve to date the fireplace [7]. Although Anne may have gone to St James's sometimes with the King while he was supervising the building of the new palace (one account of her coronation in 1533 states that, after the ceremony, she joined the King at 'his manor of Westminster' and spent the night there) there is no record of her having lived there. After her marriage to Henry she took over Baynards Castle from Catherine as a residence of her own; so she, like the King, would have had no need for a new palace.

A more likely theory is that St James's was intended to provide a Court for Henry's illegitimate son, Henry Fitzroy, who was 12 years old when the hospital was acquired [8]. He was the son of Elizabeth Blount, one of Queen Catherine's Ladies in Waiting, and his birth in 1519 gave great joy to the King, who wanted above all to have a male heir. Catherine had borne him six children, three of them boys, but all but one (the future Queen Mary I) had been stillborn or had died in infancy. Young Henry was taken away from his mother, who was then respectably married off and became Lady Tallboys, and was brought up in secret until 1525, when he was publicly acknowledged as the King's son and created Duke of Richmond. He was also, at the age of six, appointed Lord High Admiral, Lord Lieutenant of Ireland, and Lord Warden of the Marches, two of which titles his father had held before acceding to the throne. As Lord Warden he was given his own Court at Pontefract Castle in Yorkshire with a

[8] right
Henry Fitzroy, Duke of Richmond, by Lucas Hornebolte, *c.*1534.

[9] opposite
Conjectural plan of the palace as it may have been at the end of Henry VIII's reign, 1547.

household of 245 courtiers and servants, and he nominally presided over the Council of the North. There he inherited his father's passion for hunting, and was given a pack of bloodhounds by his cousin King James V of Scotland. But in 1529 his father, having heard that he was neglecting his studies, recalled him from the North and settled him at Windsor with a new tutor, to whom the King wrote, 'I deliver to you my worldly jewel: bring him up in virtue and learning.' Young Henry spent a few months at King's College, Cambridge, and then returned to Windsor, where he lived for two years with the 13-year-old Earl of Surrey (who later won fame as a poet) as his companion and close friend. In 1532 the two boys were invited by King Francois I of France to spend a year at his Court to complete their education, and on his return to England

in 1533 the young Duke, now aged 14, was married to Surrey's sister, Lady Mary Howard. By this time the building of St James's Palace was well under way, and at some point in the next two years the young couple took up residence there.

Early in 1536 Anne Boleyn (who had given the King a daughter, the future Queen Elizabeth I, but no other children) was accused of adultery, convicted of treason and beheaded. The King, with the help of Thomas Cromwell, then had a new Act of Succession passed through Parliament which declared that both his marriages were invalid, that both his daughters – Mary and Elizabeth – were illegitimate and that he himself was empowered to name a successor if he had no legitimate heirs by future marriages. It seems to have been generally expected that he would use this power to declare Henry Fitzroy legitimate and designate him as his heir; but hardly had the Act of Succession been passed than the young Duke, who had been ill for some time, died of tuberculosis at St James's Palace – the first member of the Royal Family known to have lived there, and the first to die there. By this time his father was already married to his third wife, Jane Seymour (who had been a Lady in Waiting to both Catherine of Aragon and Anne Boleyn) and in 1537 she gave birth to a son (the future King Edward VI) thus solving the problem of the succession; she died only two months later.

In an account of things done during his time in Henry VIII's service, written in 1536, Thomas Cromwell recorded that the King had 'newly builded… St James in the Fields, a magnificent and goodly house'. Cromwell himself, or perhaps Hans

Holbein the Court painter, may have been involved in designing it, with the work being carried out under the supervision of James Needham, who was Surveyor of the King's Works. But Henry evidently took a close personal interest in the building plans for all his houses, and frequently changed them. There are unfortunately very few records of the building process: the earliest surviving building accounts date from the same year (1536) by which time most of the work must have been completed. These accounts record the purchase of 70,000 bricks, 23 loads of lime, 110 loads of sand, 100 plain tiles and other materials, and the payment of wages to 7 freemasons, 13 carpenters, 22 bricklayers, 5 plasterers and 43 labourers. They may have been building the great Gatehouse, which still stands at the bottom of St James's Street and which is one of the oldest surviving parts of the

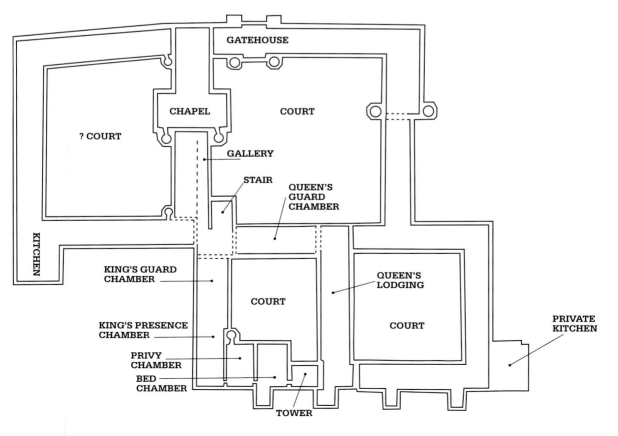

palace. The doorways on either side of the main gate bear the initials 'HR' instead of those of Henry and one of his Queens which are found elsewhere in the palace; and it is tempting to conclude that this was done during the years 1537 to 1540, when there was no Queen (Jane Seymour died in 1537 and Henry did not marry Anne of Cleves until 1540). This must have been one of the last major works at the palace during Henry's reign, since the accounts which have survived for the years 1541 to 1547 show expenditure of little more than £100 a year.

Although we have no record of what the palace looked like in Henry's time, more of his building survives than at most of his other palaces, and we can form a general idea of the layout [9]. The main entrance was through the Gatehouse to the north, and this led into a large courtyard, now called Colour Court, much of the brickwork of which is original [10]. To the west of the Gatehouse is the Chapel Royal, possibly built on the site of the 'principal hall' of the old hospital – this would explain why the chapel faces north instead of east as is normal. The Chapel Royal may indeed have been an afterthought, since one of the odd features of this part of the palace is its lack of symmetry: one might have expected the Gatehouse to lead to the centre of the main courtyard instead of being almost in one corner. Perhaps this has something

to do with the fact that the stone tower of the old hospital, which according to contemporary sketches of the palace was not pulled down until the reign of Elizabeth I (1558–1603), stood immediately to the South of the Chapel Royal, at the corner of Colour Court. To the south of Colour Court were two smaller courtyards, around which, on the first floor, were the Royal Apartments overlooking the park, which were probably the first parts of the palace to be built. These courtyards are now merged into Friary Court, and since this is now open to Marlborough Road, some of the original brickwork can clearly be seen there [11]. There may have been another courtyard to the west of Colour Court, though no trace of the Tudor brickwork remains.

The Gatehouse, now called the Clock Tower, remains very much as it was when Henry built it (apart from the clock, which is obviously later) [12]. The Chapel Royal has changed a good deal over the years, but the splendid ceiling – believed to have been designed by Holbein – is very much as it was in Henry's time [13]. The decorations on the ceiling tell an interesting story – they were clearly designed to celebrate Henry's marriage in 1540 to Anne of Cleves. Holbein had been sent by the King to Flanders the year before to paint a portrait of Anne for Henry to see before he committed himself to the marriage, which had been recommended by Cromwell for foreign policy reasons. On the strength of what must have been a flattering portrait, the King duly proposed marriage and the ceiling of the Chapel Royal was painted with the initials 'H A', with the royal arms and those of the Duke of Cleves. Unfortunately, when Anne arrived in England Henry was repelled by her appearance (he referred to her as 'the Flanders mare') and although he went through with the marriage, he divorced her five months later and embarked on his fifth marriage, to Catherine Howard. Holbein therefore had to add the Howard arms to the ceiling, while retaining those of Anne. The arms of the Prince of Wales, in honour of Henry's son (the future King Edward VI), also appear.

[12] left
The Clock Tower.

[13] opposite
Holbein's painted ceiling in the Chapel Royal, with the initials 'H A' for Henry VIII and Anne of Cleves (his fourth wife) and the arms of the King, the Duke of Cleves, Catherine Howard (Henry's fifth wife) and Edward VI. (The new Golden Jubilee panels in the ceiling are reproduced on page 149.)

34

To the south of the Chapel Royal, beyond a stone archway which may mark the site of the tower of the old hospital, a stairway led from the great court to the Royal Apartments. The layout of these apartments in all Tudor palaces tended to follow a standard pattern: on the King's side of the apartments the first room was the Guard Chamber, where the Yeomen of the Guard controlled access; then came the Presence Chamber, which contained the Throne and where the Sovereign gave audiences and sometimes dined in state. Beyond this was the Privy Chamber, to which access was much more tightly restricted, where the Privy Council would often meet and where much of the business of the Court was transacted; and beyond that the Bedchamber. The Lord Chamberlain presided over the Presence Chamber, while the Privy Chamber and Bedchamber were looked after by 18 Gentlemen led by the Groom of the Stole. (The 'Stole', or 'close-stool', was a large upholstered wooden box containing a pewter pot into which the King relieved himself; it was kept in a Stole Room off the Bedchamber, and the Groom of the Stole had the duty of being present whenever the King used it and of supervising its emptying afterwards – he was thus the King's most intimate, and therefore most influential, attendant.) A similar succession of rooms was laid out on the Queen's side.

Only three rooms from the Tudor Royal Apartments at St James's have survived – the rest were destroyed by fire in the nineteenth century. The first is the Armoury, which is the old King's Guard Chamber and which still provides access to the State Apartments [14]; the second is the Tapestry Room, which was the King's Presence Chamber [15]; and the third, now known as the Guard Room, is at right angles to the other two, and was probably the Queen's Guard Chamber. All three overlook Friary Court, and it is from the balcony outside the Tapestry Room that royal proclamations are read by Garter King of Arms.

The demolition of the old hospital must have been carried out gradually during the building of the palace, for it was not until 1536, when most of the latter was completed, that the four surviving inhabitants of the hospital were pensioned off. Following the death of the Duke of Richmond, the next regular occupant of the palace seems to have been Thomas Cromwell, perhaps so that he could keep a close eye on the completion of the building works. Much of his correspondence between 1537 and 1540 is dated from St James's, and two Ambassadors from the Lutheran Princes of Germany who visited London in 1539 reported that Cromwell had received them at 'the King's Palace at St James'. He, too, however, did not enjoy the palace for long: in 1540 he was arraigned for treason and beheaded, perhaps partly because of his role in arranging the ill-fated marriage of the King and Anne of Cleves. Thereafter the King himself used St James's occasionally, distributing the Royal Maundy in the Chapel Royal in 1543 and installing new Knights of the Garter there in 1545. Prince Edward probably stayed there from time to time before he succeeded his father in 1547 – he had his own household at Hampton

[14] opposite above
The King's Guard Chamber (now the Armoury), by Charles Wild.

[15] opposite below
The King's Presence Chamber (now the Tapestry Room), by Charles Wild.

Court, but does not seem to have had apartments at Whitehall Palace until he became King, so St James's may well have been his London base [16]. The Spanish Ambassador, writing in 1553, described the palace as having been 'built by the late King Henry as a residence for the royal children', and as late as 1588 – when there was no prince living – part of the palace was still called 'the Prince's Lodging'. So it may well be that St James's Palace was originally intended to be what it has often been since: the London residence of the Heir to the Throne.

When he became King, Edward VI used Whitehall Palace as his main residence in London, and although he frequently moved between other palaces such as Hampton Court, Greenwich and Woking, he does not seem to have spent much time at St James's. His uncle and guardian, the Duke of Somerset (brother of Jane Seymour), had apartments at St James's, and so did the Duke's younger brother, Thomas Seymour. It was at St James's that the latter, who was highly ambitious, persuaded the young King to give his blessing to his marriage to the Queen Dowager, Catherine Parr (Henry's sixth wife), who also lived at St James's from time to time. Thomas tried unsuccessfully to have himself appointed guardian to the King in place of his elder brother, and curried favour with Edward by giving him extra pocket money, but he went too far when Catherine Parr died and he began to court the young Princess Elizabeth: Somerset had him arraigned for treason and executed.

Edward does not seem to have made many changes at St James's during his short reign (he died in 1553): expenditure on the palace amounted to no more than £20 a year, and even during the reign of his half-sister, Mary I, little more than £100 a year was spent [17]. Both Mary and Elizabeth I made frequent use of St James's as a peaceful retreat from the busy life of the Court at Whitehall – Henry had surrounded the palace and its park with a wall, and it therefore provided greater security than Whitehall during times of trouble. Mary had lived there sometimes during Edward's reign, and it seems to have been her favourite residence. She had spent much of her late teens and early twenties (when she had been declared illegitimate by her father) living in seclusion in small manor houses round the country rather than at Court, and may well have felt more at home in St James's than at Whitehall. It was from St James's that she set out in September 1553, after Edward's death, to spend the traditional few nights in the Tower of London before her coronation. Throughout her reign she held meetings of her Privy Council there, particularly during times of crisis, such as the rebellion of Sir Thomas Wyatt in February 1554 against her plan to marry King Philip II of Spain (Wyatt and his followers marched past St James's on their way to the City, where the rebellion was defeated), and during the war with France in 1557–58 which resulted in the loss of Calais in January 1558. It is reported that, humiliated by this defeat, Mary said that when she died the word 'Calais' would be found engraved on her heart. A few months later she again repaired to St James's, already seriously ill, and she died there in November 1588. Her

body lay in state in the Chapel Royal for four weeks after her death, and according to one report her heart was removed and interred there before her embalmed body was taken to Westminster Abbey for burial.

Elizabeth I, like her father and her half-brother, travelled frequently between her various palaces, and Greenwich was undoubtedly her favourite, but she too stayed at St James's from time to time [18]. She made a good deal of use of St James's Park for exercise – there are frequent references in the Surveyor's accounts to the erection of gates, bridges and stiles 'for Her Majesty's walk'. There are a number of records of her staying at the palace, most notably during the approach of the Spanish Armada in 1588. She held a number of War Councils there, and it was from St James's that she set out to travel to Tilbury, where she made her famous speech to her troops ('I know that I have the body of a weak and feeble woman, but I have the heart and stomach of a King, and of a King of England too'). The last mention of St James's during her reign was in 1593, when she took Holy Communion in the Chapel Royal on Easter Day. This was an occasion of great ceremony, with three bishops, the whole Privy Council 'in their Colours of State', and earls and barons in attendance; and the organ was played by Dr John Bull, the distinguished composer and one of the pioneers of contrapuntal music.

Elizabeth spent a little more on the fabric of St James's than either of her predecessors. The main innovation during her reign was the introduction of a new water supply in 1571. Henry VIII had had a conduit house built some distance away

– roughly where the church of St James Piccadilly now stands – with pipes bringing water to the palace. This was replaced by a new conduit house immediately to the north-east of the palace, shown in a drawing from 'Cunditt Meadows' which probably dates from the late sixteenth century [19]. Water came into the conduit house through lead pipes from another conduit house near Hyde Park Corner, and from there to a 'great new cistern' in the palace itself. The only other expenditure of any importance during Elizabeth's reign was in 1581, when the lodgings of the Queen, the Lord Treasurer and other courtiers were redecorated, the ponds cleaned, and other preparations made for the reception of the Court. These works were undertaken to prepare for the visit of Francois, Duke of Anjou, the younger brother of King Henri III of France, with whom Elizabeth conducted a protracted negotiation about a possible marriage, and who stayed in London – almost certainly at St James's – for three months from October 1581 until the Queen finally gave up the idea of marrying him.

When Elizabeth died in 1603, then, the palace still largely retained the form in which it had been built 70 years earlier. It was still a subsidiary palace, providing lodgings for a number of courtiers, as well as serving as an occasional royal residence, but with no member of the Royal Family living there for any length of time. Moreover, since the accession of Edward VI there had been no Heir Apparent – the question of the succession was very much an open one throughout the Tudor period – and the role of St James's as residence for the Heir to the Throne was therefore in abeyance. All this was to change on the accession of James I.

[17] opposite above
Mary I, after Anthonis Mor.

[18] opposite below
Elizabeth I when Princess, attributed to William Scrots, *c.*1546.

[19] below
Wenceslaus Hollar's view of St James's Palace, with Westminster Abbey in the background and the Conduit House in the foreground, probably dates from the late 16th century.

3

THE EARLY STUART KINGS AND THE COMMONWEALTH

[20] previous page
James VI of Scotland and I of England, after Paul van Somer, *c*.1620.

[21] opposite
Henry, Prince of Wales in the hunting field, with Robert Devereux, third Earl of Essex, by Robert Peake, *c*.1605. Henry, standing, dressed in green hunting costume and wearing a jewelled George, has dismounted from his horse to deliver the *coup de grâce* to a stag, whose antlers are held by the kneeling Earl of Essex. Essex, who was the son of Elizabeth I's favourite, was a close friend of the Prince, but grew up to be Captain General of the Parliamentary Army at the beginning of the Civil War in 1642.

Despite all his efforts, in and out of wedlock, to ensure the succession of the Tudor dynasty, Henry VIII's family died out with Elizabeth I and the throne passed to King James VI of Scotland, whose great-grandfather, James IV, had married Henry's sister, Margaret [20]. So, in May 1603, James came from Edinburgh to London, followed soon after by his Queen, Anne of Denmark, and two of their three children – Prince Henry, aged nine, and Princess Elizabeth, aged seven. (The three-year-old Prince Charles, the future King Charles I, was too ill to travel with the rest of the family and did not come south until towards the end of 1604). For the first time in living memory, England had a Royal Family, and the English gave them a warm welcome.

The following year, having himself taken up residence with his Court at Whitehall Palace, the new King gave instructions that St James's Palace was to be the residence of Prince Henry as Heir to the Throne [21]. For the next five years the Prince seems to have spent much of his time at three of the royal palaces in Surrey – Richmond, Nonsuch and Oatlands – but during this time a considerable number of new works were undertaken at St James's to provide for his amusement. The first requirements were for a stable and barn, for Henry was from his earliest youth a keen and skilled horseman. Within a few days of the Prince's arrival the Lord Treasurer authorised the expenditure for building new stables for him, not at the palace itself but as an extension of the Royal Stables at Charing Cross, which until the early nineteenth century took up the whole of the site now occupied by Trafalgar Square and the National Gallery. At St James's a large 'shoveboard table' was built for the Prince to play on, five duck-houses were erected on an artificial island in the lake in the park, two pheasant-houses were built in the garden to the east of the palace and a little artillery house was put up in the orchard, with a cannon for the Prince to shoot at a target. It was probably at this time, too, that a Real Tennis court was built in front of the palace, on what is now the corner of Pall Mall and St James's Street. It is not shown in Hollar's drawing (see page 39), but it is mentioned in the description of the palace by a member of Marie de Medici's household in 1638 and it appears in Faithorne and Newcourt's map of 1658 [22].

According to his Treasurer and biographer, Sir Charles Cornwallis, Prince Henry had by the age of nine abandoned 'those childish and idle toys usual to all of his years' and had begun 'to delight in more active and manly exercises, learning to ride, sing, dance, leap, shoot at archery and in pieces, to toss his pike, etcetera, whereof all these things… he did wonderfully perform'. King Henri IV of France sent him a riding master, Monsieur de Saint-Antoine, and in 1607–09 a large riding-house – probably the first of its kind in England – was built for the Prince to the west of the palace, approximately on the site of what is now the guardroom in Engine Court. It survived until about 1730 and can be seen in Kip's 'bird's-eye' view of the palace drawn in 1705 (see page 56). Prince Henry also began to take an interest in books, and when the noted collector Lord Lumley died in 1609

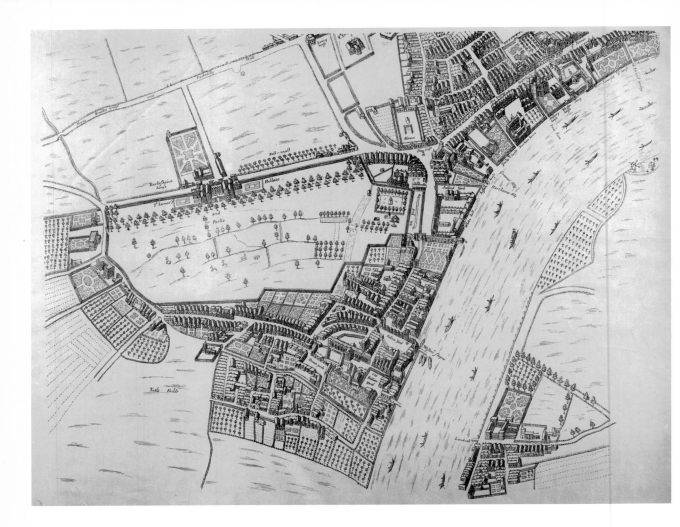

[22]
Detail from Faithorne and
Newcourt's map of London
in 1658, showing the
tennis court and a farm at
the bottom of St James's
Street, opposite the palace.

King James bought his extensive collection
of books and manuscripts for the Prince's
benefit and fitted up part of St James's as a
library to house not only this collection but
also the Royal Library amassed by previous
Sovereigns. The library was on the first
floor to the east of the Royal Apartments,
in the part of the palace destroyed by fire
in 1809.

In June 1610, when he was 16 years
old, Prince Henry was installed as Prince
of Wales, and from then on St James's
was his main residence, though he still
spent a good deal of time at Richmond,
where he was employing architects and
garden designers to embellish the palace.

But it was from this time that there first
came into being what might be called a
'Court of St James's'. Henry maintained
a large household (it numbered 426, of
whom 295 received regular salaries) and
he entertained on a lavish scale. Shortly
before his installation, he entertained his
parents and the whole of their Court to a
feast following a tournament during which
he had fought for five hours with pike and
sword. There was, however, a marked
contrast between his Court and that of
his father. Henry drew up a set of rules
for his household, specifying the duties of
each of its members and enforcing strict
discipline. Banquets and feasts were to be

conducted 'with decency and decorum, and without all rudeness, noise or disorder', unlike the drunken orgies presided over by the King at Whitehall. There was a swear-box into which anyone in the Prince's household using foul language was obliged to pay a fine, the money being afterwards distributed to charity; and the whole household had to attend church twice a day. It was a cultivated Court: many of the Prince's advisers and friends had spent time on the Continent, and through them he became familiar with the latest trends in art and architecture. He began to collect paintings, and the long gallery at St James's between the Guard Room and the Chapel Royal was fitted out and panelled to display them. In 1611 the Venetian Ambassador reported that the Prince was 'paying special attention to the adorning of a most beautiful gallery of very fine pictures ancient and modern, the larger part brought out of Venice'. Outside the palace, the Privy Garden was adorned with ten new arbours, and the orchard with a carved wooden staircase. The Prince's Works establishment spent nearly £1,600 in 1611/12, though details of what it was spent on have not survived. His Surveyor of Works at this time was Inigo Jones, who was later to become the most celebrated architect of his time; but his main task for the Prince was to design masques , a popular form of Court entertainment, for which Ben Jonson usually wrote the scripts. Inigo Jones does not seem to have built anything of note until after the Prince's death.

Prince Henry's glittering Court survived little more than two years, for in 1612 he died of typhoid fever at the age of 18. His funeral procession from St James's to Westminster was over a mile long, with some 2,000 mourners, so that the end of the procession was still at St James's as the head arrived at the Abbey. The chief mourner was Henry's younger brother, Charles, now aged 12, who had also been living at St James's. Charles had idolised his brother – who nonetheless teased him unmercifully – and Henry's death, followed soon after by the marriage of his sister, Elizabeth, to the Elector Palatine and her departure for Germany, left him lonely and miserable. His mother took little interest in him, and his father's increasingly blatant homosexuality and the debauchery of his Court repelled him. King James at first insisted that he should live with his parents at Whitehall, but not long afterwards he was given a modest Court of his own and returned to St James's. Here he lived relatively quietly until he was 18, studying and learning to fence, shoot and ride; he had inherited his brother's riding master, Monsieur de Saint-Antoine, who is shown in Van Dyck's famous equestrian portrait [23]. Charles also began to collect paintings to add to his brother's collection. The only major changes to the structure of the palace during this period were the installation of a sewer and the erection of a buttery (a storehouse for wine and provisions), which was a substantial two-storey brick building in the Palladian style near the riding-house to the west of the palace. It was almost certainly designed by Inigo Jones, who had by this time been appointed Surveyor of the King's Works, but no trace of it remains and it seems to

King that the Infanta would require a Catholic chapel when she came to London. Plans for chapels at Somerset House and at St James's were accordingly submitted for the Ambassador's approval, and after demanding some alterations he approved the plan for St James's. The Ambassador and his son laid the foundation stones for the new chapel in 1623. It is the only major addition to the palace to survive from the early Stuart period and has remained substantially unaltered since it was built, apart from work to repair the damage done to the interior during the Commonwealth period, and to the exterior during the Second World War. It was built of brick, like the Tudor palace, but rendered with ashlar – an early example of a technique usually associated with the Regency period. The Palladian design may well have echoed that of the Buttery at the other end of the palace. The coffered ceiling and cornice, gilded by Matthew Goodrich, are original, as is the Royal Closet in the gallery at the west end, with its stone chimney-piece designed by Inigo Jones; this was where the Queen was to worship. Below the gallery, on either side of the west door, are two small doors in the panelling which conceal two stones painted with consecration crosses: these may well be the stones laid by the Spanish Ambassador and his son.

Soon after work had begun on the Queen's Chapel the Spanish marriage negotiations broke down – to the relief of most people in Britain who were increasingly opposed to a Spanish alliance – and Charles returned to St James's exasperated by the way in which the Spanish Court had conducted them.

have been demolished before the end of the century – it does not appear in Kip's 1705 drawing.

A much more important addition to the palace was what is now known as the Queen's Chapel, built by Inigo Jones at the east end of the palace [24]. This owed its origin to the negotiations for Charles's marriage to the daughter of the King of Spain, begun by King James with a view to maintaining neutrality in the Thirty Years' War – by balancing his daughter's marriage to the chief Protestant protagonist with his son's marriage to a Catholic. Charles was despatched to Madrid with the King's chief minister, the Duke of Buckingham, to carry these negotiations forward, and meanwhile the Spanish Ambassador persuaded the

He showed his displeasure by entertaining, in the very rooms prepared for the Infanta, Count Ernst von Mansfeld, the German mercenary who had come to England to recruit troops to fight for the Elector Palatine against the Spanish in the Thirty Years' War. He then embarked on negotiations for a marriage with the French King's sister, Henrietta Maria, and in 1624 a marriage treaty was signed which gave the bride freedom to practise the Catholic religion in England and to have Catholic chapels in her official residences. Work on the Queen's Chapel proceeded apace and was virtually completed by the time of King James's death in 1625. Charles married Henrietta Maria by proxy in May of that year and she arrived in June with a large French retinue, including no fewer than 28 priests.

On his accession to the throne King Charles moved to Whitehall Palace, leaving St James's for the use of his Queen [25]. Their marriage seems to have been under strain from the start and they spent a good deal of time apart. It was at St James's that Henrietta Maria gave birth to five of their children, including the future King Charles II in 1630, Princess Mary – who was to marry the Prince of Orange and become the mother of King William III – in 1631, and the future King James II in 1633. During her residence at the palace the Queen had a certain amount of building and redecoration done: soon after her arrival she had a Music Gallery built in the Presence Chamber where she entertained her guests, and a wooden balcony outside the Privy Chamber next door; and her Bedchamber was decorated with a frieze.

In 1628 the King made an important addition to the Royal Collection by purchasing a large number of paintings and classical sculptures from the Duke of Mantua, and to accommodate the latter a Sculpture Gallery was erected in the Orchard to the east of the palace, where the gardens of Marlborough House are today. He also commissioned a number of sculptures by Le Sueur, Fanelli and others. Most of the paintings were hung at Whitehall, but some joined Prince Henry's collection in the Long Gallery at St James's.

In 1638 the Queen's mother, Marie de Medici (having been ordered to leave Paris by her son Louis XIII), invited herself to stay in London and arrived with a suite of 600. She was accommodated at St James's, and it is from a member of her entourage, the Sieur de la Serre, that we have the earliest detailed account of the palace. He described it as 'very ancient, very magnificent and extremely convenient'. The Great Gate was at the end of a long street (St James's Street) bounded by houses on one side and a tennis court on the other. From the 'very extensive' first courtyard a staircase ascended to the Guard Chamber and the Presence Chamber, both of which de la Serre described as being hung with beautiful tapestries, and beyond them the Privy Chamber and Bedchamber. The Long Gallery he described as 'a place designed for a private walk, where the mind may be deliciously diverted by the number of rare pictures with which its walls were covered', including Van Dyck's equestrian portrait of the King. Outside, de la Serre noted two 'grand gardens, one with parterres bordered with a box hedge'

[25]
Henrietta Maria, studio of Sir Anthony Van Dyck, 1636.

[26]
Charles I walking across
St James's Park to his
execution at Whitehall,
30 January 1649.

(presumably the garden between the palace and the park), and the other 'bordered on each side with an infinity of fruit trees' (the Orchard to the east), with 'a long covered gallery grated [sic] at the front where one may admire the rare wonders of Italy in a great number of stone and bronze statues'. To the south, de la Serre recorded that in the park King James I had established a menagerie 'filled with wild animals'. Both gardens (the parterre in altered form) and the park are visible in Kip's 1705 drawing (see page 56).

Virtually the whole of the palace must have been made available to the French Queen Mother and her retinue, for according to de la Serre no fewer than 50 separate apartments had been allocated to them. They were not popular guests: there were several anti-popery riots outside the palace during their stay, and by 1641 they had so outstayed their welcome that Parliament, at the King's request, voted £10,000 to Marie de Medici on condition that she left the country at once. After considerable delays she finally departed in September of that year and took up residence in Cologne.

In January 1642, a few months before the outbreak of the Civil War, the King and Queen with their three elder children left London for Hampton Court, but the two younger ones, Elizabeth (aged seven) and Henry (aged two) were left at St James's in the care of the Earl of Northumberland. In 1644 Parliament took control of the palace and the royal children, and set up a committee to be responsible for 'St James's House' and to dispose of many of the contents; jewellery was sold to pay for

ammunition for the Parliamentary armies, and gold from the regalia was melted down and part of the proceeds used to pay the sailors of the Parliamentary navy. In 1646, when Parliamentary forces had captured Oxford, the 14-year-old Prince James (the future King James II) was brought to St James's to join his younger brother and sister, but two years later – after two unsuccessful attempts – he managed to escape. Having organised a game of hide-and-seek with his sister and brother, he locked up the pet dog who always followed him, and used the game to creep out of a back door where he was met by a loyal colonel, dressed in girl's clothes, and smuggled on board a ship for Holland, where he joined his sister, the Princess of Orange. The Parliamentary army then took over most of the palace as a barracks, and the two younger royal children were moved to the Earl of Northumberland's home at Sion House.

At the beginning of 1649 King Charles was brought as a prisoner to St James's to stand trial at Westminster Hall, and after he had been sentenced to death the two young children were brought from Sion House to St James's on 29 January to say goodbye. Princess Elizabeth, now aged 13, left a moving account of this last meeting with their father, who urged the children to be loyal to their brother, Charles (soon to become King), and warned the eight-year-old Henry that the Parliamentarians might try to set him up as a puppet king ('They will tear me in pieces first', said the little boy). After a tearful farewell, the children were taken back to Sion House and the King spent his last hours in prayer in the

Chapel Royal with the Bishop of London. Next morning he was led across the park to Whitehall for his execution, pausing on the way to point out a tree which had been planted by his brother Henry [26].

For the next 11 years St James's served as a barracks and a prison. The Council of State took possession of the remainder of its contents, and most of the Royal Art Collection was sold: the King of Spain and Cardinal Mazarin were eager buyers, and many of the treasures in the collection ended up in the Prado and the Louvre. Some of the sculpture was moved to Whitehall where Oliver Cromwell, the Lord Protector, had taken up residence, and it may be at this time that the sculpture gallery in the garden was demolished – it does not appear in Kip's 1705 drawing. Fortunately, however, the collection of books, manuscripts and medals from the library at St James's was preserved and stored in the Queen's Chapel. The intention was to place them in a public library, but this did not happen until the books and manuscripts were presented to the British Museum by King George II – they are now beautifully displayed in the new British Library. Soldiers were accommodated at the palace and in the tennis court and riding house, and a good deal of damage was done to the fabric. Finally in 1660, after the collapse of the Protectorate and the abdication of Oliver Cromwell's son Richard, General Monck, Commander of the Parliamentary army in Scotland, marched his troops to London to restore the Parliament which had been dismissed by a military junta, and established his headquarters at St James's. The Parliament then dissolved itself and new elections were held which led to the restoration of the monarchy in the person of King Charles II.

4

THE LATER STUARTS

The troops who moved out of St James's at the time of the Restoration had left it in poor condition, and a team of bricklayers, carpenters and plasterers were soon employed to restore it for royal habitation. Charles II had taken up residence in Whitehall Palace, and so at first did his brother and heir presumptive, James Duke of York [27, 28]. Both were bachelors when they arrived, although Charles had already had five illegitimate children by four separate mistresses, and James's mistress, Anne Hyde – daughter of Lord Chancellor Clarendon – was pregnant. The Lord Chancellor's anger at this development was somewhat assuaged when James and Anne were secretly married shortly before the baby was due, but their son died at Whitehall very soon after his birth. In 1662 Charles became engaged to a Portuguese princess, Catherine of Braganza, and to make more room in the Royal Apartments at Whitehall the Duke and Duchess of York moved into St James's and took over the Royal Apartments on the south side of the palace overlooking the gardens and the park. The Duchess occupied the rooms in which her mother-in-law, Henrietta Maria, had lived, and these were lavishly decorated and provided with a flight of stairs from the balcony into the gardens. The Duke's apartments seem to have been in a new building to the west of the old Royal Apartments, the extension with three pairs of windows on the principal floor which appears in the forefront of Kip's 1705 drawing [29]. This was the first substantial addition to the Tudor palace, apart from the Queen's Chapel. It must have been built early in Charles II's reign, and may have been designed by Sir Christopher Wren, who became the King's Surveyor of Works in 1669. From these apartments the Duke conducted much of his business as Lord High Admiral. Samuel Pepys, as Secretary to the Admiralty, records in his diary a number of visits there and described the Duke's 'withdrawing-room' as one of the noblest and best-proportioned rooms he had ever seen.

The Duke and Duchess of York used St James's as their main London residence and lived there in considerable state. Soon after they moved in the Venetian Ambassador described a sumptuous banquet which they had given for the King and the Queen Mother, Henrietta Maria, who had just arrived from France; and another French visitor described the Duke and Duchess as being 'better lodged than the King and Queen'. In 1661 stables were built for the Duke's horses at the west end of the palace, where Stable Yard House now stands. Later, when he became king, a plan was drawn up to move the whole of the Royal Mews from Charing Cross to this site, but this was never carried out. The main part of Green Cloth Court, immediately to the west of the Chapel Royal, probably also dates from this period; it presumably housed the offices of the Board of Green Cloth, a department of the Royal Household responsible for auditing accounts and making arrangements for royal travel. Elsewhere in the palace a nursery was established, probably on the north side of Colour Court, where the Duke and his brother and sister had lived as children, and here were born the Duke

St James House

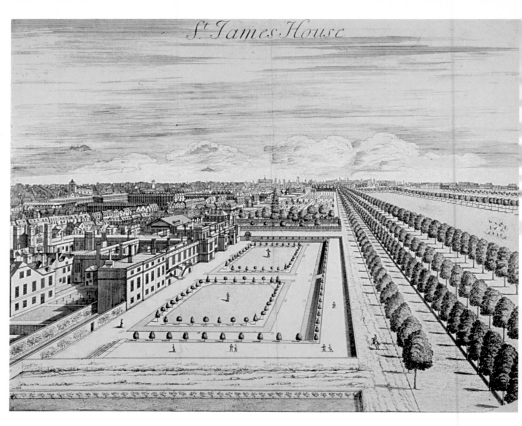

and Duchess's three children – a daughter (the future Queen Mary II) in 1662, a son, James, in 1663, and a second daughter (the future Queen Anne) in 1665. All three children were in due course given apartments of their own, but young James survived only until 1667. There were two further sons and two daughters, all born at St James's, but all of them died in infancy. Other parts of the palace were lived in by senior courtiers, royal mistresses and household staff. Pepys was a frequent visitor to Sir William Coventry, the Duke's secretary, in his apartment, and at least two of Charles II's mistresses – Hortense Mancini (Duchess of Mazarin) and Louise de Kerouaille (Duchess of Portsmouth) also had apartments; so no doubt did some of the Duke's mistresses, since at least two of them bore the inappropriate title of Maids of Honour to the Duchess.

Duchess Anne died in 1671, and two years later the Duke married again. His new bride, Mary of Modena, was Roman Catholic, and by this time James himself was making no secret of the fact that he too was a Catholic. In 1673 Parliament passed the Test Acts which made it illegal for a Roman Catholic to hold any civil or military office, and the Duke was obliged to resign as Lord High Admiral. Queen Catherine of Braganza was also Catholic, and began to use the Queen's Chapel as a place of worship. The chapel needed some restoration after it had been used to store the Royal Library during the Commonwealth. A new domed choir was installed at the east end, with the Queen's arms – the Stuart arms impaled with those of Portugal – above the east window [30]. Behind the chapel, where the west wing of Marlborough House now stands, a cloistered friary was built to house a group of friars whom the Queen summoned from Portugal [31]. Samuel Pepys was present when the Queen attended Mass in the chapel for the first time in 1662, and five years later he visited the new friary and admired the library, the refectory and the monks' cells, which all looked south over the gardens. The friary was partly destroyed by fire in 1682, and when it was being restored, the interior of the chapel was embellished under the supervision of Sir Christopher Wren; the work included the carving by Grinling Gibbons of the altar and the screen in front of the Royal Closet. The friary buildings were given by Queen Anne to the Duchess of Marlborough in 1709, and demolished to make room for the building of Marlborough House.

Mary of Modena bore four children to the Duke of York while they were living at St James's, but they all died in infancy. When James succeeded to the throne in 1685 he moved to Whitehall but gave St James's to his Queen as an official residence, and some rooms in her apartments were adapted to form a new Council Chamber, designed for her by Wren. The only other addition of importance to the palace during James II's reign was the installation in the King's apartment of the first water-closet, a 'Stool Room' with white Dutch tiles, brass fittings and ivory handles, flushed by means of a cistern and a pump. This innovation presumably made redundant, at least at St James's, the ancient office of Groom of the Stool, which from then on was a sinecure.

In June 1688 Queen Mary was expecting another child, and wished it to be born in the tranquillity and security

A 1690 view of the palace from the south, showing the part of the palace containing the Royal Apartments which was destroyed in the fire of 1809, with the Queen's Chapel in the background and the friary building on the right.

of St James's rather than at Whitehall. She stayed at Whitehall while some redecoration was carried out in her apartments at St James's, but moved into the palace on the evening of 9 June, where, the following morning, Trinity Sunday, she gave birth to a son, James. The King was of course delighted at the birth of an heir, and knighted the Queen's doctor on the spot, but his delight was by no means shared by the public at large. James had made himself very unpopular by appointing a number of Roman Catholics to senior posts in defiance of the Test Acts, but his subjects had consoled themselves with the thought that both the King's daughters by his first marriage, who were next in succession, were staunch Protestants, and that the Queen, all of whose previous children had died in infancy and who had been in poor health for some time, seemed unlikely now to be able to produce an heir. The news that she had done so caused widespread

consternation, particularly when the Pope was chosen as one of the godparents of the new prince. Rumours quickly spread that the Queen's baby had died and been replaced with another baby, smuggled into her bedchamber in a warming-pan. Bishop Burnet, in his *History of his own Times*, gave a detailed account of the circumstances surrounding the birth and came to the conclusion that the rumours were true; and a book published in 1689 by one Simon Burgis even contained a detailed plan of the palace purporting to show the route by which the replacement baby was brought via a secret staircase into the Queen's bedchamber. Despite firm denials by the King the rumours were given credence by Princess Anne, who had been absent in Bath at the time of the birth, and who persuaded her elder sister, Mary, that the new baby was a fraud. Both sisters were now married, Mary to Prince William of Orange, and Anne to Prince George of

Denmark. Both had expected to succeed to the throne and were reluctant to accept that they had been supplanted by a new half-brother.

The birth of a Catholic heir to the throne, and the measures which King James had taken to strengthen the position of Catholics in England, now led a number of leading Protestant politicians to think in terms of removing the King. They had for some time been in secret correspondence with the Prince of Orange, whom they saw as the champion of the Protestant cause. William had a claim to the throne as a grandson of Charles I (whose daughter Mary had married William's father), and his wife Mary was first in succession if the new-born prince could be excluded. In July 1688 matters came to a head, and seven leading Protestants signed a letter to William inviting him to come to England and pledging their support. William set sail in November and landed with a substantial army at Torbay in Devon, where he was duly joined by a number of Protestant peers and by several members of King James's Court, including his son-in-law, Prince George of Denmark, his nephews the Duke of Grafton (an illegitimate son of Charles II) and Lord Cornbury (son of Queen Anne Hyde's brother), and his best general, John Churchill, the future Duke of Marlborough. Finally, Princess Anne escaped from Whitehall in disguise and went to join her husband and her brother-in-law. James sent his Queen and his baby son (known to history as 'the Old Pretender') to safety in France, and left London for Rochester; a few days later he too sailed for France, and the

'Glorious Revolution' was accomplished [32]. William moved in to St James's Palace and in January 1689 summoned a Convention consisting of members of the House of Lords and of Charles II's last three Parliaments. He let it be known that he was not prepared to act either as Regent for the absent James or as Consort for his wife as Queen; and after much debate the Convention resolved that James had vacated the throne and offered it jointly to William and Mary [33]. Once this was settled, Mary – who had remained in Holland – joined her husband at St James's, and they were formally proclaimed as King William III and Queen Mary II.

The new King suffered from asthma, and the three months he had spent at St James's without outdoor activity had had a bad effect on his health. A few days after his accession he moved to Hampton Court and found the air there so much more agreeable that he decided to spend most of his time there, coming to London only for meetings of the Council and other formal occasions. He never again lived at St James's (he bought instead Nottingham House in Kensington, where the air was cleaner, and which became Kensington Palace) and for the first seven years of his reign the old palace was lived in only by courtiers. The Lord Chamberlain's records for 1692 show that there were some 50 households there, occupying about 150 rooms. The Marquess of Carmarthen (better known as Lord Danby, who had been Charles II's chief minister and was now President of the Council) occupied the Royal Apartments; the Earl of Scarborough (another of Charles II's senior courtiers who was now

a Gentleman of the Bedchamber) had a suite of twelve rooms in Colour Court; and other residents included the Duchesses of Mazarin and Portsmouth (Charles II's mistresses), several other superannuated courtiers or their widows, and a whole array of Maids of Honour, Chaplains and more junior Court servants such as the confectioner, the Page of the Backstairs, the gardener and the closet keeper. Henry Purcell, who was organist of the Chapel Royal, had an apartment in the Clock Tower above the Great Gate until his death in 1695, and the poet John Dryden lodged with him there several times to evade his creditors.

It was not long before St James's became once again a royal residence. In 1694 Queen Mary II died with no surviving children, and it was therefore certain that Princess Anne, her sister, would succeed to the throne. The following year King William offered St James's to Princess Anne and her husband, Prince George of Denmark, so that she could keep Court there 'as if she were a crowned head' [34, 35]. Several residents of the palace, from Danby downwards, were given notice to quit and Anne made the palace her principal London residence until she

[32] opposite
Mary of Modena, second wife of James II, embarking for her flight to France in July 1688 with the infant Prince James, who became known as 'the Old Pretender'.

[33] below
William III and Mary II, by Romeyn de Hooghe.

succeeded to the throne, and thereafter used it frequently for ceremonial occasions and for entertaining. Soon after she moved in she had a Ballroom built immediately to the north of Prince Henry's riding-house, on the south side of Green Cloth Court; it was connected by a hall known as the Matted Hall to the gallery which led from the Royal Apartments to the Chapel Royal (see floor plan on page 72). The Ballroom is still there, though now called the Banquet Room, and the rainwater heads on the façade bear the date 1697. A grand Court Ball was held there in 1698 to celebrate the King's birthday.

Much more extensive changes to the palace were made soon after. In 1698 the great rambling Whitehall Palace, which had been the Sovereign's principal London residence since Henry VIII's time, was destroyed by fire, leaving only Inigo Jones's Banqueting Hall. William III had not, of course, lived in the palace, but had used it for Council meetings, Drawing Room receptions and other formal occasions, and many of his courtiers had apartments there; it had also been the main seat of the Chapel Royal. Its destruction, therefore, put great pressure on accommodation at St James's, which from then until the reign of George III became the main royal palace in London. The Chapel Royal at St James's was enlarged and repaired, and from then on became the principal home of the royal choral establishment; and the Bishop of London, as Dean of the Chapels Royal, was provided with a house within the palace complex (seen next to the riding-house in Kip's drawing on page 56). The Queen's Chapel ceased to be used for

Roman Catholic worship, and was made available to Dutch- and French-speaking congregations, being renamed the 'French Protestant Chapel'. The King continued to spend most of his time at Kensington, Windsor or Hampton Court, but used the Royal Apartments at St James's when he had to come to London. Soon after the Whitehall fire he entertained Tsar Peter the Great at St James's, but the latter was clearly not impressed: after a visit to Greenwich Hospital, which was then being built by Sir Christopher Wren, he advised the King to move his Court there and to turn St James's into a hospital.

In the same year, 1698, Princess Anne's son, Prince William Henry, Duke of Gloucester – the only one of her children to survive infancy – was given his own apartments in the south-west corner of the palace, where his grandfather, James II, had lived when Duke of York; but he died only two years later at the age of 11, and this block was demolished to make room for a grand new extension to the palace. King William died in 1702 and St James's became the Court of Queen Anne. Sir Christopher Wren was commissioned to design a new set of State Apartments, and the result was the new south-west wing of the palace, which can be seen in Kip's 1720 engraving [36]. Extending west on the first floor from the Queen's Privy Chamber, it consisted of a Drawing Room (now called the Entrée Room), a Council Chamber (now the Throne Room), and a smaller room for the Clerk of the Council with a staircase beyond. Confusingly, the so-called 'Queen Anne Room' – the first in the enfilade of reception rooms as they are today – was not part of this project: it was added by George IV on the site of Queen Anne's Privy Chamber and Little Drawing Room. At the same time a colonnade, most of which still survives, was built along the west side of the Great Court from the Clock Tower gateway to the Grand Staircase leading up to the State Apartments. Later in Queen Anne's reign the gallery leading from the Guard

[34] opposite above
Queen Anne, by Charles Jervas, *c.*1702–14.

[35] opposite below
Prince George of Denmark, by John Riley, 1687.

[36] below
Detail from *Vue et Perspective de la Ville de Londres, Westminster et Parc Saint Jacques*, by Johannes Kip, *c.*1720. This later Kip panorama shows Queen Anne's State Apartments, designed by Wren, which replaced the block where James II had lived as Duke of York. At the west end of the new block is a row of houses leading towards the Park; these were demolished in the early 19th century to make room for Clarence House. In the foreground is Godolphin House, where Lancaster House now stands; it looks out over Stable Yard, and Stable Yard House can be seen opposite it at the bottom left-hand corner of the picture, with Queen Caroline's Library in the foreground between the two.

Chamber to the Chapel Royal (Prince Henry's 'long gallery') was widened.

The new State Apartments were used regularly in winter. 'Drawing Rooms', at which the Queen received Ministers, distinguished foreign visitors and 'persons of quality', were held three times a week during the season in the first half of her reign – less often after 1708. Almost anyone who chose to dress up and give the appearance of being a 'person of quality' could be admitted to these receptions, though they would not actually meet the Queen unless they could find someone to present them. The Drawing Rooms were usually well attended, and were a useful meeting place: one Lord Treasurer claimed to dispatch more business at a single Drawing Room than he could in a whole week in his office. But they were evidently rather dull occasions: Queen Anne had no gift for conversation and was often crippled by gout, and several accounts of her Drawing Rooms describe her sitting at one end of the room surrounded by her Ladies in Waiting and speaking to almost no one else. Lord Chesterfield wrote that the Queen's Drawing Rooms were 'more respectable than agreeable, [with] more the air of solemn places of worship than the gaiety of a Court'; and Jonathan Swift, attending a Drawing Room at Windsor, recorded that the Queen 'looked round at us with her fan in her mouth, once or twice said about three words to some that were near her, and then she was told that dinner was ready and went out'. The Queen's husband, Prince George, though amiable enough, was equally dull: Charles II had once said of him: 'I've tried him

drunk and I've tried him sober, and there is nothing in him'.

On special occasions such as the Queen's birthday and the anniversaries of her accession and coronation, there were often balls, plays and concerts, and the Queen regularly attended services in the Chapel Royal. In 1703 she followed an ancient tradition by touching 200 people for the 'King's Evil'. (The 'King's Evil' was a common name for scrofula, or tuberculosis of the lymph nodes, a disease which was believed to be cured if the sufferer were touched by the Sovereign; the practice dated back to the reign of Edward the Confessor.) Queen Anne was the last Sovereign to perform this rite, and Dr Samuel Johnson has recorded that when he was a boy he was one of those whom she touched (he had a 'confused but somehow a sort of solemn recollection of a lady in diamonds and a long black hood'). She also held Councils and other meetings with her Ministers at St James's, and it was there that she received the English and Scottish representatives who had negotiated the Act of Union in 1706 (ratified the following year). But like William III, Queen Anne preferred Kensington, Windsor and Hampton Court; one June she remarked to Sarah, Duchess of Marlborough, that 'though St James's is in the best part of London it must be very stinking and close at this time of year'.

In 1708 Prince George died, and the Queen shut herself away in solitary mourning at St James's for most of the following winter. Her sadness and loneliness were compounded by the fact that she had quarrelled with the Duchess

of Marlborough, who had been her close friend and confidante since before her accession. Before their quarrel Sarah had persuaded the Queen to grant to her a long lease of Crown land to the east of the palace, including the orchard and what remained of Catherine of Braganza's Portuguese friary, to build a new house for herself and the Duke, and in the spring of 1709 the construction of Marlborough House was begun. Wren was originally commissioned to design it, but the Duchess soon quarrelled with him too and took over the management of the project herself. The new house was completed in 1711 and the Duchess – having failed to persuade the

Queen to extend her existing apartment in the palace to provide a more convenient access to Marlborough House – moved out of St James's altogether, stripping her apartment there of everything she could [37].

As Anne grew older (though she was only 49 when she died), and as gout made her increasingly immobile, she spent less and less time at St James's and there were fewer and fewer Drawing Rooms and other entertainments. For much of 1712 and 1713 she was either at Windsor or at Kensington, and it was at the latter palace that she died in August 1714, the last of the Stuart Sovereigns.

[37]
The Duchess of Marlborough stripping her apartment in St James's Palace, 1711.

5

THE FIRST TWO GEORGES

When Queen Anne's son and heir, the Duke of Gloucester, had died in 1700 an Act of Settlement had been passed through Parliament providing that on the Queen's death the throne would pass to the senior surviving Protestant descendant of James I: Sophia, the Dowager Electress of Hanover, whose parents were James I's daughter Elizabeth and Frederick, the Elector Palatine. Towards the end of Anne's reign there was some speculation that she might after all favour the succession of her half-brother, James Stuart (the 'Old Pretender', he of the warming-pan). British Ministers who were negotiating for a peace treaty with France in 1712–13 had held out the possibility of recognising James's claim to the throne provided he agreed to profess the Anglican faith; but this he refused to do, and from then on it was certain that the succession would pass to the House of Hanover. Sophia herself died in June 1714, less than two months before Queen Anne, and it was her son George, Elector of Hanover, who was proclaimed as King George I [38]. In mid-September 1714 the new King, who was 54 at the time of his accession, arrived in England and took up residence in St James's Palace.

A large retinue came with him from Hanover [39]. He was accompanied by his mistress, Countess von der Schulenberg, with whom he had been living openly since divorcing his wife 20 years earlier, and by their three daughters who were known in polite society as the Countess's nieces. The King's son, George (who was soon made Prince of Wales), came, too, with his wife, Caroline, and their three daughters; their son, Frederick, aged seven, was left behind for the time being in Hanover. Soon afterwards they were joined by the King's half-sister, Sophia Charlotte, and her husband, Baron von Kielmansegg, who became the King's Master of the Horse. The fact that Sophia Charlotte often travelled in the same carriage as Countess von der Schulenberg gave rise to rumours that she too was a mistress of the King. The latter was tall and thin and the former short and fat, and they were popularly known as 'the Maypole and the Elephant'. Horace Walpole (the author and son of George I's chief minister, Sir Robert Walpole) was presented to the King in the Countess's apartment at the age of ten, and recorded that she was 'a very tall and ill-favoured lady', and went on to describe Sophia Charlotte as having 'two acres of cheeks spread with crimson, and an ocean of neck that overflowed and was not distinguishable from the lower part of her body, no portion of which was restrained by stays'. They were not popular in England, but the King was clearly very fond of them and of his daughters by the Countess, and spent much time in their company.

King George also brought with him a number of other courtiers and servants, including the Countess's half-brother as Gentleman of the Bedchamber, his Private Secretary, Baron Hattorf, several members of his German Chancery to deal with Hanoverian affairs, his German tailor, two Turkish personal attendants and his dwarf. All these people were somehow found accommodation at St James's, which for the first time in its history was now the principal residence both of the Sovereign and of the Heir to the Throne. They must have

found it rather cramped. Elaborate plans were drawn up by Sir John Vanburgh for a new palace, but these were never carried out, though there were a few additions to the buildings during the reign of George I. Of these, the most important still survive today: the range of arcaded buildings to the west of the palace (now called Stable Yard House) and the Great Kitchen in what is now Ambassadors' Court.

In 1716 Nicholas Hawksmoor, who was by then Clerk of Works, was commissioned to refurbish the stables which had been built for James II when Duke of York, and to build a two-storey brick arcade to service them and to provide accommodation for grooms and coachmen. Fifteen years later the stables were moved to Charing Cross, and the arcaded building later

became offices for part of the household of Frederick, Prince of Wales (son of George II). The Great Kitchen was built in 1717–19 and is believed to have been designed by Vanburgh [40]. It was on a massive scale – the kitchen itself rises the full three storeys of the building – and there were also offices, sculleries and a large wine vault beneath. It was built at the request of the Prince of Wales, who found it inconvenient to have meals prepared both for the King's Household and his own in the old kitchen at the south-east corner of the palace.

Immediately to the south of the new kitchen was a cistern, and during George I's reign a pump was installed to bring a new water supply to the palace; this gave its name to Pump Court, soon afterwards renamed as Engine Court. At the same

time Prince Henry's riding-house and the Bishop's house next to it were demolished, and the wing containing the Ballroom was extended southwards; finally this wing was joined to the opposite wing to the north (overlooking Cleveland Row) by a new range of apartments, enclosing Green Cloth Court and dividing it from Kitchen Court. The result of all these changes can be seen in the 1729 plan of the palace, which is in the National Archives [41].

The King took up residence in the Royal Apartments on the first floor of the palace and his mistress, the Countess von der Schulenberg (soon to be made Duchess of Kendal), was conveniently installed in a ground-floor apartment (lavishly refurbished for her benefit) immediately below the King's. Her eldest daughter Petronella (who was given the title of Countess of Walsingham) had an apartment next door to the west, and a new library was fitted up to the east between these apartments and the old kitchen. King George had little patience with the pomp and ceremony traditional to the Court, and for the first few years he did little entertaining. He received his Ministers and a few other guests in a small room known as the Closet, next to his Bedchamber and reached by the Back Stairs. He usually dined alone, walked in the gardens in the late afternoon, and had supper with the Countess and her daughters, and a few other Hanoverian intimates, in the Countess's apartment. He sometimes emerged into society to dine at the homes of his Ministers or to attend the opera or the theatre, and occasionally went to Newmarket for the races, but otherwise was little seen in public except when he was moving to Kensington Palace for the spring and to Hampton Court for the summer.

The Prince and Princess of Wales, on the other hand, entertained on a grand scale in the apartments which they occupied on the east side of Colour Court. Drawing Rooms were held twice a week, and Queen Anne's Ballroom was in frequent use. Princess Caroline was a lively and intelligent lady who enjoyed conversation and games of cards, and the Prince – though somewhat duller – was an enthusiastic and accomplished dancer. London society flocked to their parties; but their Court was soon perceived by the King as a meeting-place for opponents of his Ministry, and in the summer of 1717 he evidently decided to counter this influence, and gave more entertainments himself in an effort to gain popularity. At Hampton Court he began dining in public every day and mixing more openly with his Court, and on his return to St James's in the autumn he began to hold Drawing Rooms three times a week and established a public dining table (known as the 'Green Cloth Table') where Ministers, Members of Parliament, courtiers and other members of the Establishment were entertained at his expense. At one of the King's Drawing Rooms the Countess of Dorchester, who had been one of the mistresses of James II, found herself in the company of the Duchess of Portsmouth (one of Charles II's mistresses) and the Countess of Orkney (mistress of William III) – all by this time in their seventies. Lady Dorchester is said to have remarked: 'Who would have thought that we three whores should have met here?'

[40]
The Great Kitchen, by James Stephanoff.

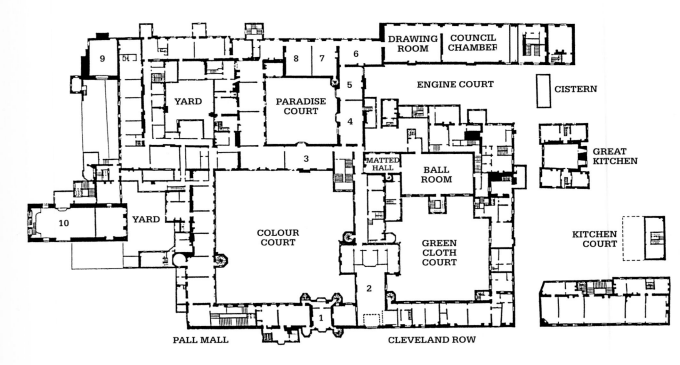

DRAWING ROOM | COUNCIL CHAMBER

ENGINE COURT

CISTERN

GREAT KITCHEN

9

8 7 6

5

YARD

PARADISE COURT

4

3

MATTED HALL

BALL ROOM

KITCHEN COURT

10

YARD

COLOUR COURT

GREEN CLOTH COURT

2

1

PALL MALL

CLEVELAND ROW

From the time of their arrival in England tension had been growing between George I and his son. When the Prince of Wales chose the Duke of Argyll as his Groom of the Stole the King forced him to cancel the appointment, because the Duke had lost royal favour by his ineffective generalship during the 1715 Jacobite rising in Scotland. The King refused to appoint his son as Regent – much to the latter's annoyance – when he paid the first of his many return visits to Hanover in 1716; and the Prince's followers in Parliament failed to support the King's Ministers on a number of important questions. Matters came to a head in November 1717 over the choice of godfathers for the christening of the Prince's second son, George. The Prince had chosen his father,

the King, as one godfather and his uncle, Ernst August, Bishop of Osnabruck, as the other; but the King insisted that the Bishop should be replaced by the Lord Chamberlain, the Duke of Newcastle. At the end of the christening ceremony the Prince publicly insulted the Duke, and the King immediately confined him to his apartments under guard. A few days later the King ordered his son to leave the palace, but said that Princess Caroline and the children would be welcome to stay provided that she had no communication with her husband. The Princess not surprisingly preferred to accompany the Prince, and they took up residence in Leicester House (in what later became Leicester Square). The children were kept at St James's, and although their mother was allowed to visit

72

them there, their father was forbidden to do so without specific permission. When the baby Prince George was taken ill in 1718 he was moved to Kensington Palace in the care of a Lady in Waiting so that both his parents could visit him; but the baby died soon afterwards and the three little Princesses remained at St James's.

The expulsion of the Prince of Wales relieved the pressure on accommodation at the palace (the new Great Kitchen could henceforth be used exclusively by the King's Household) but there were now two rival Courts. This unstable situation ended in 1720 when there was a reconciliation, with the Prince promising not to support opponents of the Ministry and the King returning to his more withdrawn way of life; but the Prince never went back to live in the palace during his father's lifetime, and although he was now able to go with his wife to visit their daughters, the latter remained very much under their grandfather's control. A young traveller from Switzerland, César de Saussure, has left an account of watching the King and Queen walking in 1725 from the Royal Apartments to the Chapel Royal accompanied by the three little princesses and their 'squires', and then attending a Drawing Room at which the Prince and Princess of Wales were both present: 'As soon as the Princess of Wales entered the drawing-room the King went to greet her, treated her most graciously, and conversed with her for some time, but he did not speak to the Prince, and even avoided going near him.' De Saussure said that, although the palace 'does not give you the impression from outside of being the residence of

a great king', he was impressed by the appearance of the rooms in which the King received his guests, with 'beautiful old tapestries' and 'excellent paintings, mostly original'. This contrast between the exterior appearance of the palace and the splendour of the interior was noted by others, though not all were impressed even by the interior: Daniel Defoe, in his *Journey through the Whole Island of Great Britain* (1724–26) wrote that 'the Palace of St James's, though the winter receptacle of all the pomp and glory of this Kingdom, is really mean in comparison with the glorious Court of Great Britain. The splendour of the nobility, the wealth and greatness of the attendants, and the real grandeur of the whole Royal Family, outdo all the Courts of Europe, and yet this palace comes beneath those of the most petty princes in it'; and the secretary to the King of Prussia, Baron Bielfeld, described it in 1749 as 'crazy, smoky and dirty'.

George I, with the Duchess of Kendal, spent much of the summers of 1719, 1720, 1723 and 1725 in Hanover, where he was reunited with the members of his family who had remained there, including his elder grandson, Frederick, and his brother, the Bishop of Osnabruck. In 1725, according to Horace Walpole (a notorious gossip whose testimony cannot always be relied on), 'their foreign Sovereign paid the nation the compliment of taking an English mistress' in the person of Miss Anne Brett, who was lodged next door to the Duchess of Kendal. When the King set off again for Hanover in 1727 Miss Brett gave instructions for a door into the gardens to be installed in her apartment; but the King's eldest daughter, Princess Anne, disliked the idea of meeting

Miss Brett during her walks in the gardens and had the door bricked up again. Miss Brett had the temerity to countermand this order, but at that point there came the news that the King had suffered a stroke in his carriage on his way to Osnabruck and had died shortly after his arrival there; and Miss Brett thereupon lost her influence and her apartment.

The new King was at Richmond with his three youngest children – a son, William (the future Duke of Cumberland), and two more daughters, all born after the Prince's expulsion from the palace – when the news came of his father's death. He and Queen Caroline immediately returned to Leicester House to prepare for the formalities of the accession [42]. He was proclaimed as George II at St James's, but did not take up residence there until the late autumn; neither he nor his Queen liked the palace, which became more inconvenient and less impressive as the years went by, particularly in comparison with other royal residences in Europe. But although Kensington, the only other surviving London palace, was delightful in summer, it was impossible in winter because of the state of the road into central London: Lord Hervey, writing from Kensington in November 1736, described the road as 'so infamously bad that we live here in the same solitude as we should do if cast on a rock in the middle of the ocean'. So the Royal Family and their courtiers and servants were obliged to squeeze into St James's from November to April every year.

When George II moved into the Royal Apartments he followed tradition by installing his mistress, Mrs Henrietta Howard, in the ground-floor apartment previously occupied by the Duchess of Kendal. He visited her there punctually at nine o'clock each evening, and it is clear that Queen Caroline was fully aware of these assignations and was prepared to tolerate them; not so Mr Howard, who on one occasion appeared in Colour Court and loudly demanded – in the hearing of the guards and others – that his wife should be restored to him. He was forcibly removed, whereupon he sent to the Archbishop of Canterbury a letter for his wife, summoning her to return to him. The Archbishop delivered the letter to Queen Caroline, who had the malicious pleasure of handing it over to Mrs Howard. The latter preferred to stay with the King, so her husband (as Horace Walpole put it) 'sold his noisy honour and the possession of his wife for a pension of twelve hundred a year'. Mrs Howard was rewarded for her fidelity to the King by being made Countess of Suffolk.

The King's elder son, Frederick, now Prince of Wales, had been living in Hanover ever since his grandfather and his parents moved to London, officially so that he could familiarise himself with his Hanover inheritance and provide a continuing royal presence to the people of Hanover, but in fact because his parents intensely disliked him (George II is recorded as having said: 'My dear firstborn is the greatest ass, and the greatest liar, and the greatest *canaille*, and the greatest beast in the whole world, and I heartily wish he was out of it') [43]. George I, before his death, had conspired with one of his daughters, now Queen of Prussia, to marry Frederick to her daughter, Wilhelmina, the

Prince's first cousin; but neither Frederick himself nor his father had been consulted about this plan, and when George II came to the throne he gave orders for the wedding to be postponed (it never came off, and Wilhelmina was eventually married to a German princeling). Frederick was finally allowed to come to England at the end of 1728, and was initially installed in the suite of apartments at the north-east corner of the palace with his sisters and his young brother, William. He almost immediately began to annoy his parents by roaming the city at night with his cronies and complaining about the size of his allowance, and before long a group of politicians hostile to Sir Robert Walpole's ministry were gathering round him. Relations between him and his parents were soon as bad as they had been between his father and his grandfather.

Frederick's eldest sister, Princess Anne, was married to the Prince of Orange in 1734 in the German Lutheran Chapel, as the Queen's Chapel was now known [44]. A large boarded gallery with an orange roof was erected for the wedding, to connect the palace with the chapel, and remained there for several weeks because the bridegroom was unwell and had to repair to Bath to take the waters before the marriage. This greatly incensed the irrepressible Duchess of Marlborough, whose windows at Marlborough House were obscured by the gallery; 'I wonder', she cried, 'when my neighbour George will take away his orange-chest'. Meanwhile, the search was on for a bride for Frederick. Various German and Danish princesses were considered, and the Duchess of

Marlborough – to spite the King and Queen – nearly persuaded the Prince to marry her granddaughter, who curiously enough was called Lady Diana Spencer; but eventually the King proposed that Frederick should marry Princess Augusta of Saxe-Coburg, and the Prince (having first despatched a valet to inspect her) readily agreed.

In preparation for the marriage Frederick was at last provided with apartments of his own. A new extension to the palace was built on the north side of Kitchen Court, at the west end of the palace overlooking Cleveland Row. The site had been partially occupied by the Guards' 'suttling-house' (where their food and drink was stored), and may have been chosen because it was as far away as possible from the apartments of the Prince's parents. The new block was fitted out as an apartment for the Prince and Princess of Wales, and is now known as York House [45]. Prince Frederick and Princess Augusta were duly married in April 1736 in a private ceremony in the Chapel Royal, after which they were installed in their new apartment, where in accordance with the German custom the Court was invited to see them sitting up in the marital bed before they were left in peace.

There are stories that the King and Queen hoped that Prince Frederick and Princess Augusta would be childless, so that their second son, William, could succeed to the throne. Whether or not there is any truth in this, Frederick and Augusta concealed the fact of the latter's pregnancy until three weeks before the baby was due in the summer of 1737; and when the Princess

[43]
Frederick, Prince of Wales, British School, *c.*1745.

Georgio II.do Mag: Brit: Franc: & Hiber: Regi

Nuptiæ Ceremoniales inter Annam Mag: Brit: Principissam Regalem et Gulielmum Principem
Arausionensem habitas in Capella Regia S.^{ti} Jacobi apud Londinum Martis 14.to An:1733.
Devotissimus et obligatissimus servus Gul: Kent.
Humillime offert, dicat, dedicatque.

[44] above
The marriage of Princess
Anne, daughter of King
George II, to the Prince
of Orange in the Queen's
Chapel, 1734.

[45] opposite
Ambassadors' Court in 1900,
showing the façade of York
House on the right.

went into labour her husband hustled her
into a coach at Hampton Court (where
the Court was in residence) and drove with
her to St James's so that the baby could be
born in their own apartment (they got there
just in time, after what must have been a
horrendous journey). The King and Queen
were wakened to be told that the Princess
was in labour and on her way to London,
and they were furious. Queen Caroline

immediately left for St James's in the middle
of the night, and having been introduced
to her new granddaughter, returned to
Hampton Court. When she returned nine
days later to visit the baby, she and her son
refused to speak to each other, though as
she was leaving Frederick knelt and kissed
her hand for the benefit of onlookers in
Cleveland Row.

The King determined to punish his son
for what he perceived as a gross insult, and
on 10 September he wrote accusing him
of 'extravagant and undutiful behaviour'
and instructing him to leave the palace
with his family as soon as the Princess's
condition allowed. So, for the second
time in 20 years, a Prince of Wales was
expelled from the Court, in this case never
to return. The Prince and Princess, with
their baby daughter (also named Augusta),
first moved to Kew, and then the Duke
of Norfolk placed his house in St James's
Square at their disposal. It was there that
their eldest son, the future King George
III, was born in 1738, but soon after the
family moved to Leicester House where
the Prince set up a rival Court, just as his
father had done in 1717. Prince Frederick
spent much of the rest of his life engaged in
political opposition to his father's Ministers;
he eventually died of pleurisy in 1751.
Meanwhile, his apartments in St James's
were given to his brother, William, Duke
of Cumberland. William studied chemistry
in his youth and had a laboratory installed
on the ground floor of his apartments to
conduct experiments; but this was ruled
to be too dangerous, and it was removed
in 1738. William later became a soldier
and was hailed as a hero in England (and

reviled in Scotland) for his victory over the Young Pretender, 'Bonnie Prince Charlie', at the Battle of Culloden, and his brutal suppression of those who had joined him in the 1745 Jacobite Rebellion.

One other change in the structure of the palace during George II's reign has survived to the present day. This was at the other – eastern – end of the north range, overlooking Pall Mall. The first-floor apartments to the east of the Clock Tower had traditionally been the children's quarters, and it was here that the young princesses lived. But against the palace walls there were a number of outbuildings – a barber's shop, the Duke of Marlborough's coach-house and an alehouse. The stench coming from the latter, and from a 'necessary house' (public lavatory) attached to it, penetrated to the Princesses' apartments, and in 1736 the 'necessary house' was demolished. In 1748 the leases of the remaining outbuildings expired and they too were demolished, and a plain two-storey building was erected to tidy up this corner of the palace. A bow window and a third storey – still visible today – were added after the accession of George III, when his own children were accommodated in these apartments.

A third addition to the palace during George II's reign has not survived. This was Queen Caroline's library, built by William Kent in 1736–37 [46]. The Queen, unlike her husband, had a taste for books and intellectual company, and the new building was designed as a retreat for her from the tedium of the Court and the squabbling of her family. It was on the site of a store-yard to the west of the palace,

overlooking Green Park, and was a single-storey building in the shape of a double cube, richly ornamented on the inside with a moulded cornice and with arched recesses for the Queen's books. Sadly, the Queen had little time to enjoy it: she was taken ill in her library only a few weeks after it had been completed and she died shortly afterwards, urging her husband to marry again ('Non, j'aurai des maîtresses' was his reply) and refusing to allow Prince Frederick to come and pay his last respects. The library was little used after her death, and it was pulled down in 1825 to make room for the new house built for George III's second son, Frederick Duke of York (now known as Lancaster House). Two of the chimney-pieces from the library, decorated with heraldic badges, were re-installed in the State Apartments, one in the Throne Room and one in the Entrée Room.

For the rest of George II's reign there were no significant changes to the palace. Very soon after the Queen's death the King fulfilled his promise to her on her deathbed by installing his Hanoverian mistress, Madame Walmoden, in the ground-floor apartment beneath his own, which had previously been occupied by his English mistress, the Countess of Suffolk (the latter had fallen out of favour and departed in 1734). Life at the Court of St James's continued in its somewhat dull routine, with Levées and Drawing Rooms at which the King spoke to almost no one, cards in the evening with Madame Walmoden (who became Countess of Yarmouth) and the occasional ball. George II lived on until 1760, and was 77 when he died.

6

GEORGE III

On George II's death the throne passed to his grandson, George, now aged 22. He had been brought up with his parents in Leicester House, and later lived with his brother, Prince Edward, in Savile House next door. In 1756, when he reached the age of 18, his grandfather had offered him his own Household in St James's Palace, but he preferred to remain near his widowed mother, and it was at Leicester House that he was proclaimed King George III [47]. Soon afterwards he moved to St James's Palace, and it was there in September 1761 that he was married to Princess Charlotte of Mecklenberg-Strelitz (whom he had not met, but who emerged as the favourite from a list of potential brides drawn up by his Ministers). The wedding day was a testing one for the bride: having arrived in England for the first time the day before, and spent the night in Essex, Princess Charlotte arrived at St James's at about three o'clock in the afternoon and was met by the King's younger brother, Prince Edward (now Duke of York). He escorted her into the garden, where her future husband awaited her. The King then took her in to the palace where she met the rest of the family and dined with them. After dinner she was dressed in her bridal clothes (which she had never seen before) and processed to the Chapel Royal, where the wedding ceremony took place at nine o'clock in the evening. This was followed by a Drawing Room, at which she was introduced to London society, and where she played the harpsichord. The bridal couple finally retired between two and three in the morning. Next day there was another Drawing Room followed by a ball, after which it is to be hoped that the new Queen had some time to catch her breath and get to know her husband.

The following year their first child, the future King George IV, was born at St James's Palace. His public life began early: 12 days after his birth it was announced that those attending Drawing Rooms at St James's could see the baby between one and three o'clock. In the same year, 1762, George III bought Buckingham House at the end of St James's Park, and renamed it the Queen's House. It was, as he told Lord Bute, 'not meant for a palace but a retreat', and it was to be the family home. Most of the King's numerous progeny were born in St James's, perhaps because a royal birth was a semi-state occasion, usually with the Archbishop of Canterbury and the Lord Chancellor present; but the King and Queen declined to live at the palace, which the King described as 'a dust trap'. His view was widely shared: one commentator wrote in 1766 that 'the Palace of St James's is an object of reproach to the kingdom in general: it is universally condemned, and the meanest subject who has seen it laments that his Prince resides in a house so ill-becoming the state and grandeur of the most powerful and respectable monarch in the universe'. In 1768 King Christian VIII of Denmark was lodged for two months in an apartment in Stable Yard prior to his marriage to the King's youngest daughter, Princess Caroline; but when his aide Count Holcke saw the outside of the palace he is said to have exclaimed: 'This will never do! It is not fit to lodge a Christian in!' Eight years later, another critic (Sir John Fielding) wrote: 'The buildings that compose this merely nominal palace (for by all rules of architecture it has no claim to the title) are low, plain and ignoble, devoid of any external beauty to attract and fix the beholder's eye. It reflects no honour on the kingdom, and is the jest of foreigners.'

So King George and Queen Charlotte preferred instead to live in the Queen's House (renamed Buckingham Palace after George IV rebuilt it) with their growing family. But the Queen's House had no State Rooms suitable for receiving guests, and on most days when in London the King rode on horseback or drove in a carriage to St James's, which was still the 'Court', to hold Levées, Drawing Rooms, audiences and Councils in the State Apartments. These were held regularly until the King fell ill in 1788. Levées, which were for men only, were held on Wednesdays and Fridays (and also on Mondays while Parliament was in session). Court dress or uniform was worn, and anyone who wore court dress was admitted; though in practice this restricted attendance to the ruling and upper classes. Attendance was virtually compulsory for members of the Royal Family, Ministers and Members of Parliament who supported the Government, and foreign Ambassadors. The Prince of Wales was once reprimanded for missing a Levée to go hunting, and Ministers like Pitt and Lord North were always careful to send apologies if government business prevented them from attending.

The Levée began at noon, when the King arrived from the Queen's House and changed into levée clothes in the State Bedchamber. He then went into the Privy Chamber next door, where only those who held or had held high office were admitted, and from there to the Presence Chamber. Those attending the Levée formed circles round the two rooms, and the King went round the circles speaking to those whom he knew or having others presented to him. When he had completed both circuits he repaired to the King's Closet, beyond the State Bedchamber, and there received his Ministers, often holding a Privy Council. If the Levée was well attended it might be five or six o'clock before he could return to the Queen's House.

Drawing Rooms, which were for both sexes and were attended by the King and Queen and the royal children (who, like the Prince of Wales, began their attendance when they were less than a month old), were held at noon on Thursdays and after the morning service at the Chapel Royal on Sundays [48]. On one occasion in 1769 the royal children were actually the hosts at a Drawing Room, with the seven-year-old Prince of Wales wearing the Order of the Garter, his six-year-old brother, Frederick, Bishop of Osnabruck, in the Order of the Bath, and their two younger brothers 'elegantly clothed in Roman togas'. But Levées and Drawing Rooms were not purely social occasions: newly created peers, newly appointed bishops and newly promoted senior service officers would kiss hands, addresses would be presented, honours and decorations would be conferred, courtiers and Ministers intending to marry would present their future spouses and seek the King's permission, and some traditionalist couples would attend specifically to inform the King and Queen of the birth of their children. Drawing Rooms, like Levées, would last for several hours, so that for the

Plate 76

Rowlandson & Pugin del.t et sculp.t   J. Bluck sculp.

DRAWING ROOM S.t JAMES'S.

London Pub. July 1.st 1809, at R. Ackermann's Repository of Arts 101 Strand.

Painted by Rob.t Smirke   Engraved by D. Jukes   Engraved by R. C. Bolton

The attempt to ASSASSINATE the KING

On the second of August 1786. Margaret Nicholson under the pretence of presenting a Petition, attempted to stab his Majesty as he was alighting from his Chariot at the garden entrance to S.t James's Palace near Marlborough Hall but was happily prevented by M.r Tippen one of the Kings footmen, and an attendant Yeoman by whom she was secured. At the same time the Sovereign with great coolness & humanely said "I have received no injury — Do not hurt the Woman — The poor Creature appears to be insane."

After several examinations no doubt of her insanity remaining she was sent to Bethlem Hospital.

London. Published Dec.r 30.th 1786 by R. Pollard, Engraver N.o 15 Braynes Row Spa Fields

first 28 years of his reign the King spent five or six hours a day at these functions, four or five days a week, all the time on his feet and without food – and on one occasion, in 1786, after surviving an assassination attempt when a deranged domestic servant named Margaret Nicholson tried to stab him as he emerged from his carriage [49]. No wonder he was glad to return to the peace of the Queen's House, though even there he sometimes received his Ministers.

In June 1788 the King suffered the first attack of the illness which was later to incapacitate him: he suffered from severe abdominal pains, variously diagnosed at the time as 'bilious' or 'gouty', though now thought to have been the onset of porphyria. He went to Cheltenham and then to Windsor to recuperate, returning briefly to London in October. There he insisted on attending a Levée 'to show that I am not so ill as some have thought', but he was clearly weak and somewhat lame, and he returned to Windsor immediately after the Levée. From then on his attendance at receptions at St James's was much less regular. In February 1801 his illness returned: the symptoms of 1788 were repeated, but this time the King rapidly became delirious and there were fears for his survival. He was sufficiently recovered to attend a Drawing Room in March 1801, but held no more Levées at St James's after 1804, when his illness struck anew and he eventually became blind (he spent most of his time thereafter at Windsor and Kew). Drawing Rooms and Levées continued from time to time at St James's, presided over by the Queen or one of the royal princes. The Prince of Wales, who became Regent in

1811 when his father finally succumbed to madness, preferred to receive his guests in Carlton House, the mansion which he had acquired and rebuilt in flamboyant style approximately on the site of the present Waterloo Place; but the rooms there, though magnificent, were not big enough for full-scale official receptions and the Prince was obliged to use the reception rooms at St James's from time to time.

The Prince of Wales had been secretly married to a young widow, Mrs Fitzherbert, in 1785. Nine years later it was decided that he should marry officially in order to produce an heir, and his cousin, Princess Caroline of Brunswick (whose mother was George III's elder sister), was chosen as his bride. He met her for the first time when she arrived at St James's for the wedding; but unlike his parents' marriage in similar circumstances this one was a disaster from the start. Caroline was unattractive in appearance, her manners were appalling and she was said to have been totally deficient in personal hygiene. When the Prince first set eyes on her he retreated to the far end of the room and called for a glass of brandy, and when the marriage took place three days later in the Chapel Royal the bridegroom had fortified himself with several glasses of the same spirit and was scarcely able to stand. He was visibly the worse for wear at the Drawing Room which followed the ceremony, and according to his wife he spent their wedding night (at Carlton House) lying in a drunken stupor on the floor. The Prince and Princess lived together for no more than a few weeks, and although a daughter (Princess Charlotte) was born in 1796 they then lived separate lives, George

87

at Carlton House and Caroline at Blackheath [50].

The State Apartments had been redecorated in 1794 in preparation for the Prince of Wales's marriage, though they still attracted unfavourable comment. Elsewhere in the palace some new accommodation for offices and apartments had been constructed around Kitchen Court and Engine Court, where a new semicircular guardroom was built (the present guardroom on the same site was built in Victorian times). These changes are shown in the 1793 plan of the palace in the National Archives – and it shows the palace at its largest extent (see page 97). By then it was built round seven courtyards: the original Tudor Great Court (now called Colour Court), with Paradise Court and Pheasant Court to the south; Green Cloth Court, Kitchen Court and Stable Yard to the west; and Engine Court to the south of Green Cloth Court. The Royal Apartments were between Paradise Court and Pheasant Court looking south over the gardens, and the State Apartments to the west of them between Engine Court and the gardens. The palace contained four chapels: the original Tudor Chapel Royal; Inigo Jones's Queen's Chapel (called the French Protestant Chapel from 1689 to 1781, when it became a German Lutheran chapel); and two chapels for French and Dutch congregations between Colour Court and Friary Court, below part of the Royal Apartments. The rest of the palace consisted of apartments of various sizes and degrees of comfort for junior members of the Royal Family, members of the Household and servants, and a large number of offices – the Lord Chamberlain's Office, the Lord

Steward's Department, the Board of Green Cloth, the Central Chancery of the Orders of Knighthood, the office of the Master of Ceremonies, the Jewel Office, the Butter and Egg Office, the Spicery, the Ewry (where ewers and table linen were stored) and many more.

The King's uncle, William, Duke of Cumberland, lived on in the apartment built for Prince Frederick in the north-west corner of the palace until his death in 1765; and his unmarried aunt, Princess Amelia, spent the rest of her life in an apartment off Colour Court. Other apartments were used by foreign royal visitors such as the King of Denmark; Queen Charlotte's two young brothers, Princes of Mecklenberg-Strelitz; and the Prince of Hesse-Darmstadt, for whom a 'splendid Court' was held at the palace in 1770. Later in the reign, St James's became the home of three of the King's sons: William, Duke of Clarence (who came to the throne as William IV in 1830, after the death of his brother George IV); Ernest, Duke of Cumberland (later King of Hanover); and Adolphus (known as Dolly), Duke of Cambridge.

Clarence was the first to move in [51]. Prince William had been sent off to join the Navy at the age of 13, and embarked in *HMS Prince George*, where he saw naval action off Cape St Vincent. In 1781 he crossed the Atlantic and spent the winter in New York (which was still holding out against the forces of the American Revolution). He then transferred to *HMS Barfleur*, in which he visited Jamaica. He was feted everywhere, and returned to England in 1783, at the end of the war, to a hero's welcome. He then spent two years travelling in Germany with

his elder brother, Frederick, Duke of York, and later went to sea again in the frigate *HMS Hebe*. In 1786, when he came of age, he was given a house at the west end of St James's Palace, between Vanburgh's Great Kitchen and Stable Yard, more or less where Clarence House now stands. It was at the northern (left-hand) end of the row of houses seen in the foreground of Kip's 1720 drawing (see page 63), and the Duke had his sister Princess Augusta as his next-door neighbour to the south. His house was originally a bachelor establishment, fairly modest by princely standards; and in 1789 he took a house at Petersham in Richmond Park, where he installed a Miss Polly Finch as his mistress. Two years later Miss Finch was replaced by an actress called Mrs Jordan, who already had several illegitimate children and with whom Prince William had ten more in the course of their relationship, which lasted for 20 years. As a result of Mrs Jordan's efforts, the St James's Palace house was extensively and lavishly redecorated between 1806 and 1809, and she and the Duke of Clarence divided their time between it and their country house, first at Petersham and then at Bushy Park.

In 1811, however, the Duke evidently decided that he should get married in order to produce some legitimate heirs. The Prince of Wales had an only daughter, Charlotte, then aged 15; the next of George III's sons, Frederick, Duke of York, had been married for 20 years without producing any children; and it was therefore highly possible that the Duke of Clarence would succeed to the throne. So one evening in 1811, when Mrs Jordan was acting in a play at Cheltenham, she received a summons

from the Duke to meet him at Maidenhead where he told her that they must part. He offered her £4,400 a year and the custody of their five daughters on condition that she gave up her acting career; but she soon went back to the stage, the daughters rejoined their brothers at the Duke's house at Bushy, and in 1816 Mrs Jordan was obliged to flee to France to escape her creditors (she died soon afterwards).

Meanwhile, the Duke went in search of a wife – a quest made more urgent by the sudden death in November 1817 of Princess Charlotte of Wales. She had been married in 1816 to Prince Leopold of Saxe-Coburg, but she died in childbirth and her baby also died. This left the Prince Regent's three eldest brothers, the Dukes of York, Clarence and Kent, in direct succession to the throne; and Edward, Duke of Kent, now decided that he too must get married and produce an heir. He had been living for 27 years with his French Canadian mistress, Madame de Saint Laurent, but he parted from her – reluctantly – and she retired to a convent. Edward lost no time in finding a bride, and in May 1818 he was married to Prince Leopold's sister, Victoria, widow of the Prince of Leiningen; a year later a daughter was born at Kensington Palace. The Duke of Clarence was more dilatory, but after several unsuccessful attempts he finally became engaged to Princess Adelaide of Saxe-Meiningen, whom he married in July 1818. The Duke of Clarence and his new Duchess spent most of the first nine years of their marriage at Bushy Park, which the Duchess does not seem to have minded sharing with the ten illegitimate children of her husband and Mrs Jordan; but they

[51]
Prince William, Duke of Clarence, by Thomas Gainsborough, 1782.

retained the house at St James's as a town residence. The Duchess bore two daughters, but both died in infancy, so it was clear that the succession would eventually pass to the Duke of Kent's daughter, the future Queen Victoria.

Ernest, Duke of Cumberland, was the second of George III's sons to take up residence in St James's Palace, in 1799 when he returned to England at the age of 28 after commanding Hanoverian troops fighting the French in Holland [52]. He was given the suite of rooms at the west end of the palace overlooking Cleveland Row (in what is now known as York House) which had been built for his grandfather, Frederick Prince of Wales; and from 1799 to 1812 large sums were spent on the decoration of his apartment. The Duke was highly unpopular: he was a fierce martinet as an Army commander and an arch-reactionary in politics, and the facts that he was neither married nor equipped (like most of his brothers) with a well-known mistress, and that the walls of his apartment were known to be hung with mirrors, gave rise to all sorts of lurid rumours about his private life. These rumours reached a climax in 1810, when it was widely reported that Cumberland had murdered his valet, Sellis, in his apartment. It was said that the murder had been committed either because Sellis was blackmailing the Duke or because he had interrupted his master while in bed with Mrs Sellis. According to the Duke, however, Sellis had attacked him with his own sword while he was asleep, and had then locked himself in his room and cut his own throat. This version was corroborated by the Duke's other servants and by the Palace Guard, and

the jury at Sellis's inquest had no hesitation in returning a verdict of suicide, but the public was unconvinced. Cumberland was invited by his brother, the Prince of Wales, to move into Carlton House to recover from the injuries he had suffered at Sellis's hands, and his apartments at St James's were opened to the public, who were able to see the splashes of dried blood on the walls.

Not long after this incident Parliament instituted an enquiry into allegations of corruption by the Duke of Cumberland in an election in the borough of Weymouth, and in 1813 he was persuaded to leave the country and settle in Hanover. His apartment at St James's – by then the most sumptuous in the palace – was again refurbished the following year in preparation for the arrival in London of Tsar Alexander I of Russia and King Frederick William III of Prussia, with a galaxy of statesmen and generals of the allied armies, for a grand celebration of victory over Napoleon and his exile to Elba. The Prince Regent had intended the apartment to accommodate the Tsar, but the latter preferred to stay in a hotel with his sister, much to the chagrin of the Court officials who had spent the whole day in full dress waiting to receive him at the palace, with a guard of honour and two bands in full state uniform. The Tsar did, however, use the Duke of Cumberland's apartment to hold court and receive visitors; the King of Prussia was installed in the Duke of Clarence's house and Marshal Blucher – the main foreign hero of the victory over Napoleon – stayed in a house on the west side of Kitchen Court (now Ambassadors' Court), where he appeared frequently at

a window to acknowledge the enthusiastic cheers of large crowds – in those days the various courtyards of the palace were open to the public most of the time.

The Duke of Cumberland's unpopularity increased when in 1814 he announced his engagement to Princess Frederica of Solm-Braunsfeld. The Duke was already 43 and his fiancée 37, and she had not only been married twice before but had been engaged in between these two marriages to Cumberland's popular brother, Adolphus, Duke of Cambridge, whom she had jilted. King George III had made public his consent to Adolphus's engagement before Frederica broke it off, and regarded her behaviour as an insult. The rest of the Royal Family, and the British public, believed her to be immoral (many asserted that she had murdered her two previous husbands). Queen Charlotte made it clear that she would refuse to receive her new daughter-in-law; and Parliament refused to vote the customary increase in

the Duke's allowance from the Civil List on his marriage. Cumberland returned to England briefly after the wedding, but soon afterwards returned to Germany and set up house with his wife in Berlin.

Adolphus himself was the third of George III's sons to live at St James's [53]. In 1803 he returned to England from commanding the Hanoverian army, and was given an apartment on the ground floor in the south-east corner of the palace facing the park (probably where George I's and George II's mistresses had lived). The Duke lived a quiet and apparently blameless life there and at Windsor until January 1809, when he returned to his apartment from a dinner party at about two o'clock in the morning. The porter who had waited up to admit him reported a smell of burning, and a dog could be heard barking in an adjacent apartment. The Duke went to the Yeomen's guard-chamber, near the King's back stairs to the west of his own apartment, and from there he could see flames coming through a

[53] opposite
Adolphus, Duke of Cambridge, by Sir Thomas Lawrence, 1818.

[54] below
Sketch of the south-east corner of St James's Palace *c*.1710, showing the Royal Apartments which were destroyed in the fire of 1809.

window. The fire brigade was summoned, but the nearest supply of water was the canal in St James's Park and they had to relay buckets of water from there, helped by a team of boys from Westminster School. The fire had probably been burning for some time before it was discovered, and it took many hours to bring it under control. It eventually destroyed the whole of the south-east part of the palace [54], from just south of Inigo Jones's chapel on the east side to the beginning of the State Apartments on the garden front, including both the King's and the Queen's private apartments [55]. The only casualty was one of the Queen's dressers, who had gone early to bed because she had to leave for Windsor early next morning. She had taken a candle with her to bed, and this may have caused the fire in which she perished.

The King's and Queen's private apartments had hardly been used since the move to the Queen's House, so the results of the fire were not disastrous for the Royal Family, apart from the unfortunate Duke of Cambridge, who was obliged to find a new home. He spent most of the rest of his life either in Hanover, where he was Governor-General from 1813 until 1837, or at Cambridge House in Piccadilly (which was to become the Naval and Military Club). Most of the State Apartments were unaffected by the fire, and Drawing Rooms and Levées continued to be held there. But gone was a major part of the old Tudor Palace: the Great Bedchamber in which so many royal children had been born, the old Library and Kitchen, the French and Dutch Chapels, and the great warren of apartments surrounding Friary Court

and Pheasant Court. Most of the valuable paintings and furniture were saved thanks to the efforts of the firemen, the Westminster schoolboys and various members of the Household and staff who had been evacuated from their apartments, led and encouraged by the Prince of Wales and three of his brothers – an interesting parallel with the fire at Windsor Castle in 1992. But much was lost, including many books and papers from the Royal Archives. Fortunately, the major part of the Royal Library was no longer in St James's, having been given by George II to the British Museum (it is now in the British Library).

There was much debate about the extent to which the palace should be restored after this disaster, and the ruins of the destroyed apartments lay untouched for several years. John Nash, the Prince Regent's favourite architect, was invited to submit proposals for the restoration, but in 1818 he wrote to the Surveyor-General of the Office of Works that 'every part of the Palace is in such a dilapidated state that… it is not susceptible of repair, and any attempt to restore it would be attended by more expense than rebuilding it'. Three years later he wrote: 'Not only the lead of the gutters are worn out, but the boards on which they are laid – the walls are crooked and bulged and the bricks and mortar decayed – the roofs are scarcely susceptible of repair – the floors are sunk – the timbers rotten and the boards worn out – the frames of the windows are incapable of holding the glass – in short I consider every shilling laid out on the buildings as money thrown away'; but his advice was ignored, and St James's Palace was reprieved.

[55]
Plan of the first floor of St James's Palace in 1793. The section enclosed by a red line was destroyed in the 1809 fire.

1 Clock Tower
2 Chapel Royal
3 German Lutheran Chapel (now Queen's Chapel)
4 Pheasant Court
5 Duke of Cambridge apartments
6 Duke of Clarence apartments
7 York House (Duke of Cumberland)
8 Queen Caroline's Library

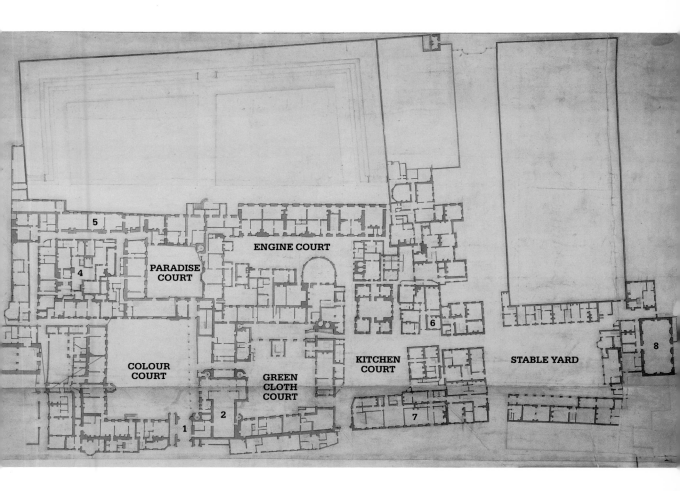

ENGINE COURT

PARADISE COURT

COLOUR COURT

GREEN CLOTH COURT

KITCHEN COURT

STABLE YARD

7

GEORGE IV AND WILLIAM IV

[56] previous page
*The Banquet at the
Coronation of George IV*,
by George Jones, 1821.

[57] opposite
The south front of St
James's Palace in 1820,
showing the gap left by the
destruction of the Royal
Apartments.

King George III, who had been living in seclusion at Windsor, died there in 1820 and the Prince Regent became King as George IV [56]. His mother, Queen Charlotte, had died two years earlier, and he then moved from Carlton House to the Queen's House. His estranged wife, Queen Caroline, had gone in 1814 to Italy, where she had a number of adulterous relationships (including a brief affair with the King of Naples), but she returned to England on hearing of her father-in-law's death. At George IV's request the Government put forward a bill in Parliament for his divorce from the Queen, but although the bill passed the House of Lords it was dropped because Caroline was for some reason widely popular and it was feared that the House of Commons would reject it. When the new King was crowned in Westminster Abbey in 1821 Caroline tried to enter the Abbey demanding to be crowned as Queen, but she was refused admission. She died a few weeks later.

George now asked his Government for funds to refurbish the Queen's House, but Lord Liverpool, the Prime Minister, told him that any funds for further building works would have to come from the sale of some other piece of Crown property, and he suggested that St James's Palace should be sold or demolished. The King replied that until the Queen's House could be redesigned St James's was still, despite its dilapidation, the only royal residence in central London with rooms spacious enough for State occasions. Thomas Pennant's 'Account of London', first published in 1820, made the same point: 'Uncreditable as the outside of St James's may look, it is said to be the most commodious for regal parade of any in Europe'.

In 1822 the King ordered 'the immediate execution of certain extensive arrangements… for the necessary accommodation of the company attending… Levées and Drawing Rooms which are in future to be held at this Palace'. So, between 1822 and 1824 a major programme of work was carried out at a cost of some £60,000. A new reception room – now known confusingly as the 'Queen Anne Room' – was built on the site of the old Privy Chamber and Little Drawing Room (see 1729 plan on page 72), and this became the first in the enfilade of State Rooms in which Drawing Rooms and Levées were held. It was aligned externally with the existing State Rooms built by Wren in Queen Anne's reign, so that the whole of the south wing of the palace appeared as a single block [57]. At the same time the buildings between Green Cloth Court and Kitchen Court were demolished, and the resulting large court renamed Ambassadors' Court. Those attending a Levée or Drawing Room in the State Apartments came through the main gate in the Clock Tower (which in those days was normally open to the public), then along the colonnade on the west side of Colour Court into an entrance hall from which Wren's Grand Staircase led them up to the Armoury and Tapestry Room, where their credentials would be examined before they could gain admittance to the Queen Anne Room. However, certain people such as Government Ministers, Ambassadors and senior judges and civil servants, had 'the

W. M. Craig Del.   Published by T. Kinnersley Feb. 14. 1820.   I. Brown Sc.

South View of St. James's Palace

Privilege of Entrée', and this entitled them to attend Levées and Drawing Rooms at any time. So, to enable these distinguished guests to avoid the queue of people waiting to have their credentials checked, a new staircase was built opposite Wren's Grand Staircase, leading up to the Matted Hall outside the Ballroom; and a new Entrée Corridor was built from there, parallel with the Armoury and Tapestry Room, leading straight into the Queen Anne Room [58]. Everything to the east of the Armoury, Tapestry Room and Queen Anne Room had been destroyed in the fire, and the resulting large courtyard was named Friary

Court. Some outbuildings between Colour Court and the Queen's Chapel were also demolished, leaving a passage through to Pall Mall which eventually (in 1856) became Marlborough Road. The results of all these changes can be seen in the 1841 plan of the palace [59].

Meanwhile, the Duke and Duchess of Clarence were complaining about the inadequacy of their house at the other end of the palace, and in 1825 the King commissioned Nash to produce a plan for a more suitable house for them on the same site. The result was Clarence House, which was erected on the site of the old

[58] opposite
The Double Staircase
leading to the State
Apartments, with the
original staircase dating
from Queen Anne's time in
the foreground and beyond
it the new staircase built
in the 1820s for the use
of those with the Right of
Entrée attending Levées
and Drawing Rooms.

[59] below
Plan of the first floor of St
James's Palace in 1841.

1 Clock Tower
2 Chapel Royal
3 Queen's Chapel
4 Double Staircase
5 Guard Room
6 Armoury
7 Tapestry Room
8 Queen Anne Room
9 Entrée Room
10 Throne Room
11 Entrée Corridor (now
   Picture Gallery)
12 Matted Hall
13 Ball Room
14 Clarence House
15 York House

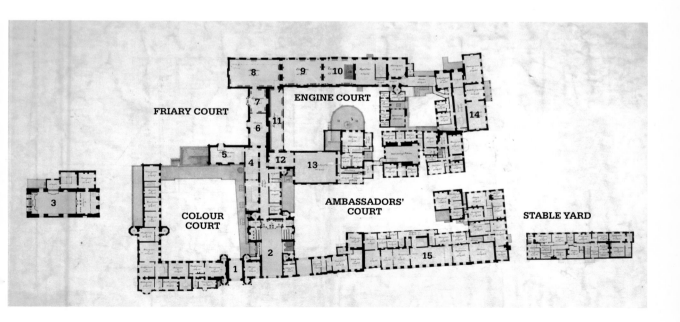

house between 1825 and 1827. In contrast
to the mellow brickwork of the palace,
Clarence House was built of stone with
a bright stucco finish; it originally faced
west into Stable Yard, with its back to
the State Apartments [60]. Construction
proved more complicated than Nash had
expected because of the need to renew and
strengthen the foundations, and because,
as usual, plans were changed several times;
and Nash's original estimate of £9,000–
10,000 was less than half the final cost.

Not to be outdone, the Duke of York,
the eldest of George IV's brothers, decided
that he must have a sufficiently grand
house to be worthy of his position as Heir
to the Throne, and one in which he could
continue to live after his accession. In

1807 he had acquired Godolphin House,
on the south side of Stable Yard, which
can be seen with its large garden in the
foreground of Kip's engraving on page
63. He now decided to demolish both his
own house and Queen Caroline's library
in order to build himself a palace, and
Benjamin Wyatt and Sir Robert Smirke
were commissioned to design it for him.
The result was a splendid mansion in Bath
stone in neo-classical style – the last great
London house to be built in this essentially
Georgian style. The lavish interior was
designed by Wyatt and Sir Charles Barry
(who built the Houses of Parliament).
It was to be called York House, but sadly
the Duke of York died in 1827 before it
was finished. The wealthy Marquess of

Stafford (later the first Duke of Sutherland), who is said to have lent the Duke £60,000 for its construction, bought it, completed it and named it Stafford House (it was renamed Lancaster House in the twentieth century) [61].

Nash had been drawing up plans for the Queen's House, with a view to making it a more sumptuous residence for the King, but on the assumption that St James's would continue to be used for State occasions and to accommodate the Household offices. However, in 1826 George IV changed his mind and decided that the Queen's House, now renamed Buckingham Palace, should replace St

James's as the 'Court'. St James's was to be demolished and replaced by a terrace designed by Nash, as a continuation of the two terraces he was building on the site of Carlton House (which had been demolished in 1825). If this plan had been carried out, Carlton House Terrace would have extended all the way to Lancaster House, and Clarence House, St James's Palace and Marlborough House would have disappeared. Once again, however, Lord Liverpool imposed a veto: Parliament, he told the King, would not agree to the demolition of St James's when so much public money had just been spent on refurbishing it. So once again St James's

[60] opposite
Clarence House in 1861, showing the original portico and entrance facing west.

[61] below
Lancaster House c.1800, originally built for Frederick, Duke of York, then acquired by the Marquess of Stafford and named Stafford House, later bought by Lord Leverhulme, renamed Lancaster House, and presented to the nation.

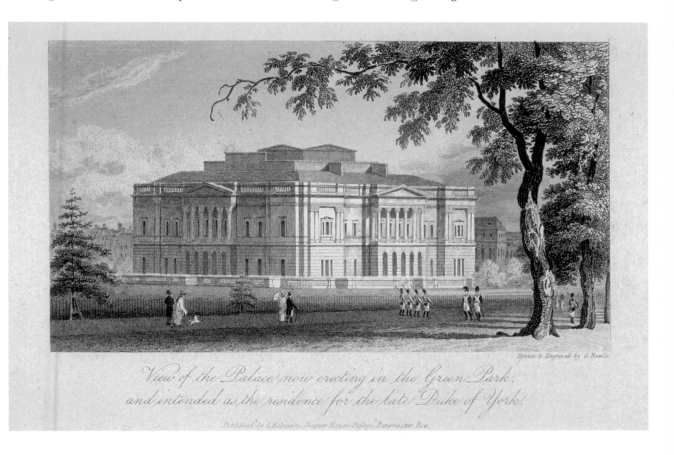

View of the Palace now erecting in the Green Park, and intended as the residence for the late Duke of York.

Published by S. Robinson, Chapter House Passage, Paternoster Row.

was spared, and in 1827 an apartment between the Duke of Cumberland's and the Chapel Royal was hastily fitted up (with, among other comforts, a shower-bath and double glazing) for the accommodation of the King himself, who lived there until the alterations to Buckingham Palace had been completed.

Meanwhile, a new water supply was installed throughout the palace, the roof of the Chapel Royal was repaired, and another large sum was expended in extending the Duke of Cumberland's apartment. The Duke himself returned from Berlin in 1829, despite the efforts of George IV and his Prime Minister (the Duke of Wellington) to dissuade him, for the express purpose of leading the opposition to the Catholic Emancipation Bill which was then the subject of heated debate in Parliament. His apartment at St James's became the meeting place for a group of extreme Tories, and he spent much time at Windsor trying to persuade the ailing George IV to oppose the Bill. In this he eventually failed, but his efforts as the effective leader of the right wing of the Tory party certainly contributed to the downfall in 1830 of Wellington's government.

George IV died in 1830, with the rebuilding of Buckingham Palace still incomplete, and the Duke of Clarence, who succeeded him as William IV, had no wish to live there (he even offered it as the new home for the Houses of Parliament, which had just burned down, and serious consideration was also given to housing the National Gallery there). William's first idea was to move into Marlborough House, which had been relinquished by the Dukes of Marlborough when the fourth Duke died in 1817. It had then been intended as a residence for Princess Charlotte, George IV's daughter, and her husband, Prince Leopold of Saxe-Coburg; but Charlotte died before moving in, and Prince Leopold lived there alone until 1831 when he was invited to become the first King of the Belgians. King William thought he and Queen Adelaide could live 'very comfortably indeed' in Marlborough House 'if he might have a passage made to unite this house with St James's', and plans were drawn up to link the two buildings with a raised gallery and to provide St James's with two new wings projecting south towards the Mall. As usual, however, these plans exceeded the money likely to be available from a Parliament still busy investigating the extravagant sums spent on Buckingham Palace, and in the end William decided to remain at Clarence House. A new gallery was built overlooking Engine Court to link Clarence House with the State Apartments. Marlborough House was assigned by the King in 1835 as a dower house for Queen Adelaide if she should survive him.

The only other changes to the palace during William IV's short reign were the restoration of the Clock Tower at the foot of St James's Street and of the Chapel Royal. In 1832 the roof and upper storeys of the Clock Tower were found to need renewal, and in the process the 100-year-old clock was removed, on the grounds that the building could not carry its weight, and taken to Hampton Court. This gave rise to an outcry from the public, and a petition was sent to the King asking for the clock to be replaced – there had been a clock in the tower for over 200 years. William was sympathetic and enquired why it was thought that a clock was too heavy for the tower when it was the custom for large numbers of people to gather on the roof to watch processions and guests gathering for Levées and Drawing Rooms. There was no answer to this, and a new clock was accordingly installed [62]. Then, in 1836, a major refit of the Chapel Royal was carried out by Sir Robert Smirke, who redesigned the Royal Closet at the southern end of the chapel, designed a new ceiling above it in the same style as the Holbein ceiling of the main chapel, and erected side galleries.

As William grew older he spent more and more time at Windsor, coming to St James's only for Levées and Drawing Rooms. He held his last Council in May 1837 in a wheelchair, and was too ill to attend the ball at St James's on 24 May in honour of the coming of age of his niece, Princess Victoria. On 20 June he died at Windsor, and his widow, Queen Adelaide, then moved to Marlborough House, where she lived until her death in 1849.

[62]
The 1832 clock on the Clock Tower.

8

QUEEN VICTORIA

On William IV's death the throne passed to Princess Victoria, only child of the Duke and Duchess of Kent, who was living with her widowed mother at Kensington Palace. She was the first sovereign since William III never to live at St James's Palace, but in accordance with tradition she went there on the day after her accession to watch the heralds proclaiming her as Queen before a large cheering crowd in Friary Court [63]. She then gave a number of audiences and held a Privy Council before returning to Kensington Palace [64]. Three weeks later she moved into Buckingham Palace – as the first Sovereign to live there in its new guise – and it was there that her first entertainments were held: a large dinner party and concert almost immediately after she arrived, and the first of many State Balls a few months later. The expansion of the palace planned by George IV and Nash, and continued by Edward Blore after Nash's dismissal, had been completed only a month before Victoria's accession, and it was clear that she intended to use it to the full.

This once again raised the question of the future of St James's, and some members of Parliament called for its demolition. In 1838 the House of Commons debated the site for the new Houses of Parliament designed by Barry to replace the part of the Palace of Westminster burned down in 1834. One MP suggested that the proposed site on the banks of the Thames at Westminster was unsuitable, would overshadow Westminster Hall and the Abbey, and would cost far too much; it would be better to use this insalubrious site for quays and warehouses, and to build Barry's design on the site of St James's Palace. Fortunately this idea was rejected; for despite all its shortcomings St James's was still considered to be the only royal residence in London suitable for the holding of Levées and Drawing Rooms.

Levées and Drawing Rooms remained an essential part of Court life. On these occasions prominent citizens (and those who aspired to prominence) were received by the Sovereign, and the height of many people's social ambition was to be 'presented at Court'. Presentation was a jealously guarded privilege and the Lord Chamberlain's Office took great pains to prevent 'unsuitable' people from being presented. In 1855 it was decreed that no native of India (not even the Rajah of Coorg) could be presented without the previous sanction of the Board of Control of the East India Company, and in the same year a peeress who wished to present the wife of her solicitor (Mr Haynes of St James's Street) was told that it was considered 'undesirable to extend the entrée to Court to members of Mr Haynes's profession… except under peculiar circumstances'. Mrs Haynes subsequently attended a Drawing Room, claiming that she had not been told of this ruling, and succeeded in getting herself presented; but when this was discovered her presentation was 'declared null and void'. In 1856 a Mrs Nicoll was refused presentation because her husband was a retail trader, but was admitted two years later after her husband had been elected to Parliament. Actors were also deemed to be 'not eligible for presentation'; this rule was relaxed in 1919, though even then it was specified that each case would be judged on its merits, and only those members of the theatrical profession who were of 'irreproachable character' could be presented.

Levées were also sometimes used for the conferring of knighthoods and other honours, the presentation of Loyal Addresses to the Queen, and other ceremonies which nowadays take place at Investitures or private audiences. Cabinet ministers were expected to attend as a matter of course (though leave of absence for business reasons was readily granted), and so were heads of foreign diplomatic missions. This could cause problems: there was a prolonged correspondence in the 1850s and 1860s between the Lord Chamberlain's Office and the United States Legation about what the American Minister should wear at Court. Diplomatic or Court uniform was *de rigueur*, but Congress had passed a resolution forbidding American diplomats from wearing uniform. In 1854 two members of the American Legation appeared at a Levée wearing trousers, and without swords: this caused consternation in the Lord Chamberlain's Office, and the two received an official reprimand. The following year the Minister agreed to go to Court in evening dress with breeches, cocked hat and sword, but in 1868 his successor was instructed by the State Department not to appear at all, and the following year the Lord Chamberlain's Office relented and allowed him to dispense with the cocked hat and sword – a privilege later extended to some South American Legations. Quakers were also exempted from wearing swords at Court.

Queen Victoria held her first Levée and Drawing Room at St James's within a month of her accession. In 1840 she was married to Prince Albert in the Chapel Royal (which was fitted up for the occasion with extra galleries both within the Chapel and in Colour Court), and thereafter Prince Albert often held Levées on the Queen's behalf until his death in 1861 [65, 66]. In 1862, with the Queen still in

The Royal Closet, St James's

Her Majesty giving audience to an Ambassador

Le Cabinet de la Reine. Sa Majesté donne audience à un Ambassadeur.

Das Königliche Cabinet. Die Königin giebt Privat Audienz einem Gesandten.

[65]
The Marriage of Queen Victoria, 10 February 1840, by Sir George Hayter, 1840–42.

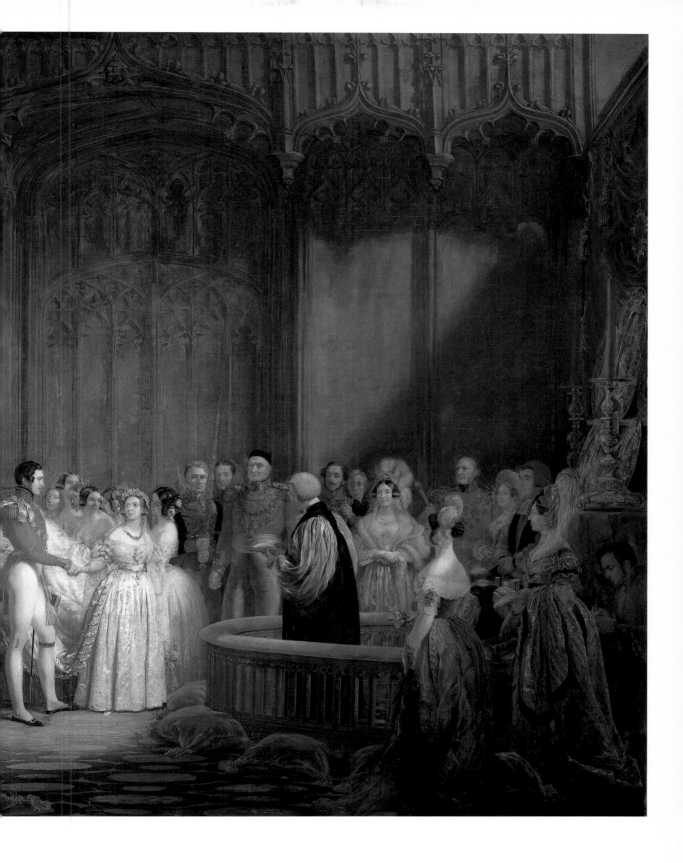

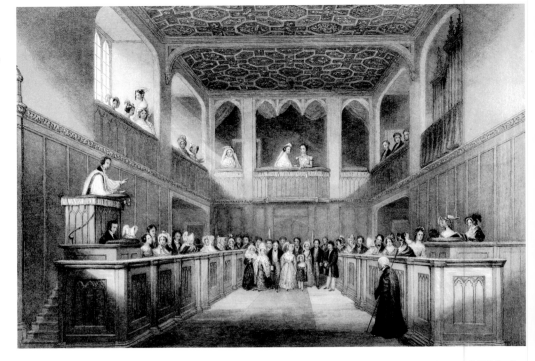

deep mourning, there were no Drawing Rooms at all, and it was announced that ladies and gentlemen who would have sought to be presented could send their names to the Lord Chamberlain, together with the names of those who would have presented them, and if all was found to be in order they would receive a 'certificate of presentation' instead. From then on Drawing Rooms were increasingly held at Buckingham Palace, where the facilities for receiving large numbers of guests had improved, but Levées continued to be held at St James's, usually by the Prince of Wales on the Queen's behalf. The Queen held her last Levée and Drawing Room at St James's in 1865.

The number of people attending Levées and Drawing Rooms was now much greater than in previous reigns – some 1,500 people came to the Prince of Wales's Levée in February 1863, and 1,000 (not counting the Court) attended a Drawing Room in May of the same year. To reduce congestion in the approaches to the State Apartments, a new staircase was built from Ambassadors' Court to the Ballroom, and those with the Right of Entrée could now use this route to the State Apartments without having to go through the crush of the entrance from Colour Court [67]. The Entrée Corridor was found to be too narrow for these new arrangements, and in 1864 it was widened to its present size; it was decorated by William Morris, who called it the Ambassadors' Room, and later it became the Picture Gallery, which is now an integral part of the State Apartments [68]. At the same time another new corridor was formed on the ground

Colour Court. St James's Palace

floor along the south side of Colour Court, through which people leaving the State Apartments could go straight out into Marlborough Road, thus further reducing congestion at the Colour Court entrance [69]. (This corridor is now the main Visitors' Entrance to the State Apartments.) William Morris and Son were again commissioned to redecorate the Armoury and Tapestry Room in 1866–67, and in 1880–82 the rest of the State Apartments, including the Visitors' Entrance and the staircases. The choice of William Morris represented remarkably early recognition by the Court of the new Arts and Crafts style of design.

In addition to Levées and Drawing Rooms, other ceremonies were held at St James's from time to time. The Queen held Investitures of Knights of the Garter

there in 1837 and again in 1839, but they have never been held there since. In 1860, after a Volunteer Force (the forerunner of the Territorial Army) had been formed to meet the perceived threat of an invasion by Napoleon III, Queen Victoria held a reception there for more than 2,200 officers of the new Force (together with 45 Lord Lieutenants); and in the same year Prince Albert attended a banquet there to mark the bicentenary of the Grenadier Guards. From then on the Queen found it more convenient to receive her subjects at Buckingham Palace, and the State Apartments at St James's were less often used, though there were two large evening parties there in 1863 to celebrate the marriage of the Prince of Wales to Princess Alexandra of Denmark. The Prince had been given Marlborough House in 1850

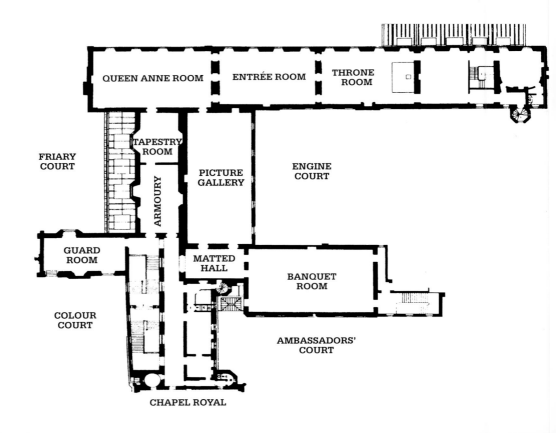

(when he was only nine years old) following the death of Queen Adelaide, but did not live there until he attained his majority (in the meantime it accommodated part of the National Gallery). Marlborough House was then enlarged and completely renovated in 1859–63, and became the official residence of the Prince and Princess of Wales. The renovation included the restoration of the splendid wall paintings representing scenes from the battles won by the first Duke of Marlborough, which had been painted over when Queen Adelaide occupied the house in 1837. The Prince used St James's Palace from time to time thereafter, holding an investiture of the Order of the Bath in 1865 and using it for dinners and meetings where the number of guests was too great to be accommodated in Marlborough House.

St James's still contained a large number of Household offices and apartments. The latter were occupied by members of the Royal Family and their staffs, and a number of retired officials and widows of officials who were granted living accommodation by 'Grace and Favour'. The largest and most sumptuous apartment, occupying most of the block between Cleveland Row and Ambassadors' Court, was that of the Duke of Cumberland, Queen Victoria's eldest surviving uncle. He had become King of Hanover in 1837, because the ancient Salic Law which still applied in Hanover banned Queen Victoria, as a woman, from inheriting the throne; and he lived there permanently from then until his death in 1851, returning to England only once for a few months in 1843. For the rest of that time his apartment remained vacant (apart presumably from some resident staff) but he stubbornly refused to give it up. In 1840, when the Queen was about to be married and the Duchess of Kent had to move out of Buckingham Palace, the Queen asked her uncle whether her mother might live in his apartment, but the King of Hanover flatly refused. After his death, his apartment was given to the recently widowed Duchess of Cambridge, Queen Victoria's aunt, who lived there quietly until she died, at the age of 91, in 1889. Thereafter, the apartment was extensively refurbished and extended, taking over a number of rooms on the ground floor previously occupied by the Robes Office and other offices, for the use of the eldest son of the Prince of Wales, the Duke of Clarence and Avondale, who had previously lived with his parents at Marlborough House. The Duke, however, died in 1892 at the age of 28 before these alterations were completed, and his younger brother the Duke of York (later King George V) moved in to the apartment, which was then renamed York House. The following year, in the Chapel Royal at St James's Palace, the Duke of York married Princess Mary of Teck (a granddaughter of the Duke of Cambridge), who had become engaged to his elder brother only a few weeks before the latter's death. Although the couple spent much time at Sandringham and at White Lodge in Richmond Park, where their eldest son (the future King Edward VIII) was born in 1894, York House was thereafter their London base where they gave a series of dinner parties for Ministers, diplomats and members of the Royal Family; and where the Duke received instruction in the British Constitution and the role of the monarchy from a Cambridge professor.

Clarence House had fallen vacant on the death of William IV, and was then made available to Princess Augusta, the eldest surviving daughter of George III. She had previously lived in the house next door, seen in the foreground of Kip's engraving (page 63). Her previous house and its neighbour to the south, Harrington House, were demolished, and the space which they had occupied became part of the gardens of Clarence House. Princess Augusta died in 1840, and this enabled Queen Victoria to solve the problem of a house for her mother, the Duchess of Kent, who lived in Clarence House until her own death in 1861. The Duchess had a small conservatory built on the south side of the house (where Princess Augusta's old house had been), with a porch which enabled her to enter and leave the house from the Mall through the gardens, instead of having to use the front door on Stable Yard Road. She also enlarged the house to the east by taking over the carpenters' shop on the ground floor between Clarence House and St James's Palace, and used the passage on the first floor above it, which William IV had used as access to the State Apartments, for her wardrobe. In 1866 Queen Victoria gave Clarence House to her second son, Prince Alfred, Duke of Edinburgh, and he in turn lived there until his death in 1900.

It was Prince Alfred who carried out (at his own expense) the alterations which resulted in Clarence House looking very much as it is today, following his marriage in 1874 to the Grand Duchess Marie, daughter of the Emperor Alexander II of Russia, who doubtless demanded something grander than the original

[70]
Prince Alfred, Duke of
Edinburgh and Marie,
Duchess of Edinburgh,
*c.*1874.

Clarence House [70]. The south front was realigned to be level with the south front of the palace, so that the two buildings appeared as a continuous whole, despite the contrast between the brickwork of St James's and the stucco of Clarence House. The old main entrance on to Stable Yard to the west was closed up, and the Duchess of Kent's conservatory was replaced with a portico, which became the main entrance to the house, with a conservatory above it on the first floor (demolished in 1948) [71]. Prince Alfred also changed the appearance of many of the rooms and installed a Russian Orthodox Chapel for his wife on the first floor (this was dismantled in 1900, but some fragments of wall paintings can still be seen) [72]. Prince Alfred died in 1900 and his widow did not wish to continue living in Clarence House. The Duke of York hoped to move there from York House, but Queen Victoria decided instead that Clarence House should go to her favourite son, Prince Arthur, Duke of Connaught, who occupied it – but seldom lived there – until his death in 1942 [73].

A third spacious apartment within the palace was in Engine Court, on the ground floor overlooking the gardens, below the State Apartments. In the 1840s it was the home of Prince George of Cambridge, who succeeded his father as Duke of Cambridge in 1850 and soon afterwards moved to his father's house in Piccadilly. Later his apartment was given, by 'Grace and Favour', to two of the Queen's nephews, Prince Ernest of Leiningen and Prince Victor of Hohenlohe-Langenburg, grandsons of the Duchess of Kent by her first marriage [74]. These two had become

naturalised British subjects and joined the Royal Navy (both rose to the rank of Admiral), and were boyhood companions and close friends of the Prince of Wales. When Prince Victor married the daughter of a British Admiral, his cousin moved out of the Engine Court apartment and it remained in the possession of Prince Victor (who was thereafter known as Count Gleichen), and after his death of his widow and his daughters, Lady Feodora and Lady Helena Gleichen. Prince Victor was a talented amateur sculptor and in 1879 his apartment was extended by the construction of a new wing on the south side of Friary Court, with a studio at the east end. The studio was later used by his daughter, Lady Feodora, who became a very well-known sculptor and the first woman to be elected (albeit posthumously) a member of the Royal Society of British Sculptors. The Gleichens' studio is still there, and was for many years used for

[71] opposite
The south front of Clarence House as it is today, with the Duke of Edinburgh's portico forming the main entrance to the house.

[72] above
Fragments of the walls of the Russian Orthodox Chapel built in Clarence House for the Duke of Edinburgh's Russian wife Marie.

the restoration of paintings for the Royal Collection; part of Count Gleichen's apartment later became the office of the Clerk of Works.

Meanwhile Stafford House in Stable Yard (originally built for Frederick, Duke of York) continued as the London home of the Dukes of Sutherland. The second Duke used its magnificent interior as the setting for a series of lavish parties: among the celebrities whom he entertained was the 'Great Liberator' of Italy, Guiseppe Garibaldi, who stayed at Stafford House during his visit to London in 1864, and the composer Frederic Chopin, who played at a Stafford House reception attended by the Queen, Prince Albert and the Duke of Wellington. The Queen is reported to have said when she went to visit the Duchess of Sutherland: 'I have come from my house to your palace.' [75]

Until the mid-nineteenth century the various courtyards of the palace were usually open to the public, and early paintings of the palace show members of the public strolling through them. In 1847 the State Apartments themselves were opened to the public, when 100,000 people came to see Winterhalter's new painting *The Royal Family in 1846* [76]. But in 1848 fears of a Chartist outbreak of violence led to the gates under the Clock Tower being closed at night, with the palace being garrisoned by the Brigade of Guards, as well as by the Sovereign's traditional bodyguards – the Gentlemen at Arms and the Yeomen of the Guard. Again in 1884, when the police reported a threat of dynamite attacks, the gates were closed and new gates were erected at the entrance to

several unprotected courtyards. Nowadays, of course, access to all parts of the palace is strictly controlled.

The 1841 Census recorded 174 people – 66 male and 108 female – as living within St James's Palace. The Rev. Edgar Sheppard, author of the first substantial history of the palace, published in 1894, listed six senior members of the Royal Household who occupied apartments, some of them quite large, in which no doubt their families and several servants also lived. There were at least another 15 apartments occupied by more junior officials, and a few still lived in – by 'Grace and Favour' – by retired officials or their widows. In fact, the palace had by the end of Queen Victoria's reign a population similar to that of a small village.

[73] opposite
Arthur, Duke of Connaught, by Rudolf Swoboda, 1888–90.

[74] below
Prince Victor of Hohenlohe-Langenburg, Count Gleichen, *c*.1891.

[75] below
*The Grand Staircase of
Stafford House* (Lancaster
House), by Joseph Nash,
*c.*1850.

[76] opposite
*The Royal Family in
1846*, by Franz Xavier
Winterhalter. The children
are, left to right, Prince
Alfred, the Prince of Wales,
Princess Alice, Princess
Helena and Princess
Victoria.

9

FOUR TWENTIETH-CENTURY KINGS

Queen Victoria's long life came to an end at Osborne House on the Isle of Wight on 22 January 1901, and on the following day the 60-year-old Edward VII held his first Council at St James's Palace, where the proclamation of his accession was read by Garter King of Arms in Friary Court on 24 January [77]. Shortly afterwards King Edward and Queen Alexandra moved to Buckingham Palace from Marlborough House, which was then refurbished for occupation by the Heir to the Throne, the Duke of York, who on his father's accession became also Duke of Cornwall and later Prince of Wales [78]. The Duke and Duchess of York had occupied York House since 1893, and during the London season they lived there regularly; but for most of 1901 they were on an eight-month tour of the Commonwealth, visiting Australia, New Zealand, South Africa and Canada, and when in Britain they spent much time in the small and gloomy York Cottage at Sandringham, of which the Duke was very fond. He never liked York House ('This is a beastly house and I think very unhealthy', he wrote to his wife), and when he moved out in 1903 it became known as the King's Visitors' House and was used to accommodate State Visitors such as President Poincaré of France, King Albert I of the Belgians and the Crown Prince and Princess of Japan. Later the Master of Ceremonies – predecessor of the Marshal of the Diplomatic Corps – was given part of York House as an official residence and office, while other rooms were used by the Lord Chamberlain's Office.

Edward VII resumed the practice of using the State Apartments at St James's, where electric light had recently been installed, for ceremonial occasions. In 1901 he held several Investitures there and received a number of Loyal Addresses, and in 1902 Levées were resumed [79]. There were no ceremonies there in 1903, however, because the State Apartments were being used as a furniture store. The King clearly had unhappy memories of Osborne House (where he had spent much of his boyhood under the strict tutelage of his father, Prince Albert) because when Queen Victoria died he lost no time in presenting it to the nation as a Naval College and convalescent home for ex-servicemen. So the furniture from Osborne was stored in the State Apartments until it could be re-allocated to other royal residences, and some furniture from Marlborough House was also stored there during the refurbishment. But from 1904 Levées and Investitures were held regularly, and the State Apartments were also made available for other purposes. In 1904 the General Officer Commanding Home District was allowed to use them for the examination of officers while the rooms normally used at Horse Guards were under repair, and in 1906 the British Red Cross was given permission to hold meetings in the Banquet Room. The latter was also used as a studio by artists making copies of the King's state portrait for distribution to government buildings and embassies abroad, and in 1909 the Honourable Company of Gentlemen at Arms celebrated their fourth centenary with a banquet in the State Apartments.

Apart from the various refurbishments of Marlborough House, York House and

the State Apartments, the only work on the structure of the palace during Edward VII's reign was the installation in 1902 of a new wine cellar adjoining Colour Court. During the excavations for its construction a lead coffin and some loose human bones were unearthed, probably dating from the time of the leper hospital.

When Edward VII died in 1910 the new King and Queen, George V and Queen Mary, moved to Buckingham Palace, and Marlborough House was again refurbished for occupation by the Queen Mother, Queen Alexandra, who lived there until

her death in 1925. The Queen's Chapel next door, which had previously been used by a German Lutheran congregation, became a Danish Lutheran chapel in 1902 (Queen Alexandra was Danish), and the congregation erected a memorial to the Queen's memory after her death, which is set into the wall of Marlborough House gardens on Marlborough Road.

George V continued to hold Levées in the State Apartments, though Investitures were more commonly held at Buckingham Palace. The Apartments were also used by various charitable organisations for

[79]
A Levée at St James's Palace, by Messrs. Dickinson, 1902–05.

meetings, and in 1912 they were for the first time made available to the Foreign Office for an international conference. A Balkan Peace Conference was convened there in December 1912 at the end of the first Balkan War between the Ottoman Empire and a coalition of Serbia, Montenegro, Bulgaria and Greece. Talks were suspended the following month following a coup in Turkey, but were later resumed and ended in May 1913 with the signature at St James's of the Treaty of London providing for the independence of Albania.

During the First World War the State Apartments were used by Queen Mary's Relief Clothing Guild, and much of York House was made available to the Prince of Wales's National Relief Fund. A furnished apartment in York House was also given to the Chief of the General Staff (Lord Kitchener until his death in 1916, and thereafter Sir William Robertson). After the war Levées and meetings were resumed. From January to April 1930 the State Apartments were the scene of a Naval Conference involving delegates from Britain and the Dominions, the United States, France, Italy and Japan which ended with a treaty whereby Britain, the United States and Japan agreed on limitations for the construction of naval vessels. In November of the same year the first in a series of Round Table Conferences on the future of India was held in the Picture Gallery. A second Round Table Conference from September to December 1931 was attended by Mahatma Gandhi, who was given as his office one of the rooms in the corridor leading from the State Apartments to the Chapel Royal [80].

The State Apartments were also used for a number of social occasions. In 1913 the King and Queen gave an evening party there on the eve of the marriage of the King's cousin, Prince Arthur of Connaught and his niece the Duchess of Fife, and after the wedding the State Apartments were opened to the public (for the first time since 1847), when some 50,000 people passed through the Banqueting Room to view an exhibition of wedding presents. In 1922 the King and Queen gave an afternoon party on the occasion of the marriage of their daughter, Princess Mary the Princess Royal, to Viscount Lascelles (later the Earl of Harewood), and similar parties were held in 1934 and 1935 for the marriages of their sons, the Duke of Kent to Princess Marina of Greece, and the Duke of Gloucester to Lady Alice Montague Douglas Scott. After each of these weddings the State Apartments were again opened for a display of wedding presents. The Prince of Wales, the Duke and Duchess of York and the Duke of Connaught also gave receptions in the Apartments and in the gardens; and in 1935 there was a Grand Silver Jubilee Reception for the Diplomatic Corps and a banquet to mark the 450th Anniversary of the Yeomen of the Guard

In 1919 Edward Prince of Wales, now aged 25 and with his own household, was given York House, and he retained it both as a London residence and as an office until well after his accession to the throne as King Edward VIII [81]. It was as gloomy a house as it had been when his parents had lived there twenty years before, and the Prince soon set about redecorating it and getting rid of the Victorian furniture. The large

dining room on the ground floor, which had been used by the Lord Chamberlain's Office before the war, was frequently in use for lavish dinner parties, and among those who occupied rooms in the rest of the house were the Prince's younger brother, Prince George (later Duke of Kent), his cousin, Lord Louis Mountbatten (later Earl Mountbatten of Burma), and his equerry and close friend, Major Edward Metcalf, always known for some reason as 'Fruity'. An increasingly frequent guest in the house was the American divorcee, Mrs Wallis Simpson, whom Edward married after his abdication. Other guests included Fred and Adele Astaire, stars of a current West End show called *Stop Flirting*, who were invited to give private dancing displays after their public performances.

In January 1936 George V died at Sandringham, and the following day the proclamation of Edward VIII's accession was read on the balcony overlooking Friary Court – and broadcast for the first time by the BBC – with the King himself and Mrs Simpson watching from the window of the Guard Room. The new King held his Accession Council and his first Levée in the State Apartments, but thereafter Privy Councils, Levées, Investitures and audiences were held at Buckingham Palace. He disliked the latter, complaining of a 'dank and musty smell' every time he set foot in it, and he went there only to do business, using an office just inside the King's Door which opens off the inner courtyard. He continued to live at York House for the first six months of his reign, and the Royal Standard was flown, for the only time in this century, from a flagpole

(since dismantled) on top of the Clock Tower. The ground-floor dining room was again used for a number of dinner parties, guests at which included Stanley Baldwin (the Prime Minister), Winston Churchill and the aviator Charles Lindbergh. In August the King went on holiday, first to the Mediterranean (cruising on a yacht with Mrs Simpson) and then to Balmoral. He stayed briefly at Buckingham Palace in October and November before his abdication in December, and he never returned to St James's; York House became the home of his brother, the Duke of Gloucester [82]. Queen Mary the Queen Mother moved into Marlborough House, and the Queen's Chapel ceased to be used by the Danish Lutherans and was restored and given over for use by the Chapel Royal.

Edward VIII's abdication, forced on him by the Government because of his determination to marry Mrs Simpson, placed a reluctant Duke of York on the throne as King George VI [83]. He had

[81] opposite
Edward VIII as Prince of Wales, by Sir Arthur Stockdale Cope, 1912.

[82] below
The Duke and Duchess of Gloucester with their sons, Princes William (left) and Richard (now Duke of Gloucester), in Australia in 1946.

Apartments on the eve of his brother's coronation in 1937, and used them for other parties when there were too many guests to be accommodated in York House.

In February 1939 the State Apartments were again the venue for an international conference, this time on Palestine. The conference was called by the British Government in an attempt to resolve the impasse between Jews and Arabs about the future of Palestine [84]. The Jewish and Arab delegations refused to sit at the same table, and discussions were held separately by the British with each delegation. At one point during the conference, the Emir Feisal of Saudi Arabia and the Emir of Yemen climbed through the Armoury window on to the balcony overlooking Friary Court in order to watch the Changing of the Guard. After six weeks of discussions the British Government put forward proposals for a solution which would limit Jewish immigration into Palestine and which envisaged the eventual creation of an independent Palestine State. These proposals were rejected by both the Jewish and Arab delegations, and the conference ended in failure.

As the threat of the Second World War drew near preparations were made at St James's: air raid shelters were constructed in the Office of Works workshop beneath the south side of the palace; the Lord Chamberlain's Office moved from Stable Yard to Frogmore House at Windsor, and their offices, along with part of the State Apartments and part of York House, were made available to the Joint War Organisation of the Red Cross and the Order of St John for the relief of prisoners

been living with his family in a house in Piccadilly (since destroyed), but after his proclamation and Accession Council at St James's he moved to Buckingham Palace. He held a number of Levées in the State Apartments at St James's until he discontinued them in 1939. The Duke of Gloucester gave a banquet in the State

of war. There were eventually over 300 people working in this organisation, and they were later described by a member of the King's staff as occupying 'every nook and cranny of the Palace'. The Queen's Chapel was closed for the duration because of structural damage after an air raid, but although the choir of the Chapel Royal was disbanded from 1940 to 1944 the chapel itself remained in use, with volunteers from the War Office supplying a choir, and weekday services were held there throughout the war for the Red Cross and St John staff and for people who had been bereaved in air raids or in battle. Much of the Royal Collection of paintings, together with the gold plate from the Chapel Royal and the Royal Marriage Register, was moved to Windsor; and even the suits of armour in the Armoury were removed in case they became dislodged and injured the Red Cross staff.

There was a good deal of bomb damage to the palace: a land mine exploded near the railings in St James's Park in October 1940, blowing out windows and doors on the south side of the palace and in Clarence House; in November a bomb was dropped in Cleveland Row, causing minor damage to York House (and temporarily disrupting telephone and power cables in the palace); and the ceiling of the Picture Gallery was cracked by vibrations from a nearby battery of anti-aircraft guns. In March 1941 the Guard Room and the top floor of York House were damaged by incendiary bombs, and in May the range of buildings on the south side of Friary Court was destroyed by a high explosive bomb. These rooms had contained the office of the Clerk of

Works and also the servants' quarters of the apartment in Engine Court still occupied by Lady Helena Gleichen, whose family had lived there by 'Grace and Favour' since Victorian times. The Friary Court building was not reconstructed until 1960, by which time the adjoining apartment was occupied by George V's daughter, Princess Mary the Princess Royal. In 1944 there was some damage to both the Chapel Royal and the Queen's Chapel: the north window of the Chapel Royal and the altar below it were destroyed, and temporary glass and a new altar were installed soon after the war; the Queen's Chapel was restored and rededicated in 1953.

In June 1941 the Picture Gallery was used for a historic meeting of Allies: Winston Churchill convened the meeting, which included Commonwealth High Commissioners in London and representatives of the Governments in exile of European countries under German occupation (Belgium, Czechoslovakia, Greece, Luxembourg, the Netherlands, Norway, Poland and Yugoslavia, with a representative of General de Gaulle, leader of the Free French). The meeting resulted in a declaration issued on 25 June in which the participants pledged to continue the

[83] opposite
George VI, by Sir Gerald Festus Kelly, 1938–45.

[84] below
The Palestine Conference held at St James's Palace, February 1939.

war effort together until final victory. The Declaration of St James's Palace, as it was called, also stated: *The only true basis of enduring peace is the willing cooperation of free peoples in a world in which, relieved of the menace of aggression, all may enjoy economic and social security. It is our intention to work together and with other free peoples, both in war and peace, to this end.* This Declaration was a major milestone on the way to the foundation of the United Nations Organisation. After this, the King gave instructions for the Picture Gallery to be kept furnished for future meetings of this kind, and another meeting of Allies was held there in September 1941.

In January 1942 the Duke of Connaught, last surviving son of Queen Victoria, died at Clarence House at the age of 92. He had spent most of his life as a soldier, rising to the rank of Field Marshal, and was Governor-General of Canada from 1911 to 1916. He had lived only for part of each summer at Clarence House since the death of his wife, Princess Louise, in 1917, and when he himself died the house was made available for the remainder of the Second World War to the Red Cross and the Order of St John, who moved there from the State Apartments. Part of the garden of Clarence House was then provided as allotments for residents of the palace to grow their own vegetables. After the end of the war in 1945 the Red Cross and St John moved out, and Clarence House underwent a major renovation between 1947 and 1949. When the renovation was completed Princess Elizabeth and the Duke of Edinburgh, who had been living in Buckingham Palace since their marriage in 1947, made Clarence

House their home [85].

Meanwhile St James's gradually returned to normal. Much war damage had to be repaired, and a good deal of refurbishment was required following the departure of the large number of Red Cross and St John's workers who had occupied much of the palace. The State Apartments were still in reasonable condition and were not redecorated until 1950; in the meantime they were used in September 1945 for a dinner for eighty delegates to the Council of Foreign Ministers, in January 1946 for a State Banquet for the delegates to the first meeting of the United Nations Organisation, in May 1949 for a Council of Europe Conference, and in May 1950 for a Government dinner for the Atlantic Pact powers. A number of other meetings and receptions were held there by charities with which members of the Royal Family were associated, and this has since become the most common use of the State Apartments. Levées had been discontinued on the outbreak of war and were never resumed, and the role of the State Apartments as a venue for international conferences was taken over by Lancaster House in Stable Yard.

Stafford House had remained the London home of the Dukes of Sutherland until 1912, when the lease was bought by the Lancashire soap magnate, Sir William Lever (later Lord Leverhulme). He changed its name to Lancaster House, after the city of his birth, and presented it to the nation as the home for the London Museum; and when the Museum moved to Kensington Palace in 1950, the house was restored for use by the Government for conferences and hospitality.

10

QUEEN ELIZABETH II

George VI died at Sandringham on 6 February 1952, and on the same day the Privy Council met at St James's Palace to make arrangements for the accession of his successor as Queen Elizabeth II [86]. The new Queen was on a visit to Kenya when her father died, but she returned to London the next day and her accession was proclaimed in the traditional way from the balcony of Friary Court on 8 February. The Queen and the Duke of Edinburgh watched the ceremony from the Tapestry Room, and Her Majesty then held a Privy Council at which she took the Oath of Accession. The royal couple continued to live at Clarence House for a few months, and it was there that they received foreign Heads of State on the eve of the late King's funeral on 15 February. A number of audiences were held at Clarence House in February and March, but thereafter The Queen and her family moved to Buckingham Palace. In May 1953 Queen Elizabeth the Queen Mother and The Queen's sister, Princess Margaret, took up residence in Clarence House [87]. Princess Margaret moved to Kensington Palace on her marriage to the Earl of Snowdon in 1960. Earlier in 1953 The Queen's grandmother, Queen Mary, had died, the last member of the Royal Family to live in Marlborough House. The house was then put in the care of the Ministry of Works, and after a major refurbishment The Queen formally handed it over to become the headquarters of the Commonwealth Secretariat.

Several members of the Royal Family have lived in St James's Palace during The Queen's reign, the most senior being Prince Charles, the Prince of Wales. In 1986 The Queen invited a firm of management consultants to review the workings of the Royal Household, and among their recommendations – all of which were accepted – was the transfer of the offices of the Lord Chamberlain from St James's Palace (where they had occupied most of York House and some other parts of the palace) to Buckingham Palace so that they could be close to, and better coordinated with, the offices of The Queen's Private Secretaries. At the same time the offices of the Prince and Princess of Wales were moved from Buckingham Palace to St James's Palace. The Prince and Princess lived at Kensington Palace, but when they decided to separate in 1995 Prince Charles moved to St James's Palace and occupied an apartment to the east of the Clock Tower, which had previously been used by the Lord Chamberlain. When his grandmother, Queen Elizabeth the Queen Mother, died in 2002 the Prince of Wales and his family moved to Clarence House.

The late Duke and Duchess of Gloucester, uncle and aunt of The Queen, continued to occupy York House until the Duke's death in 1974, when most of York House was converted for office use. Another of The Queen's aunts, the late Princess Mary the Princess Royal, occupied the apartment in Engine Court, below the State Apartments, which had been the 'Grace and Favour' home of the Gleichen family; the Princess only used it as a London base and spent most of her time at Harewood House, the country seat of her husband. The Duke and Duchess of Kent, cousins of The Queen, lived for

many years in part of York House. They have now moved to Kensington Palace, but the Duke's Household Office is still at St James's, and his sister, Princess Alexandra, now occupies the 'Gleichen' apartment. Princess Anne, the Princess Royal, and Princess Beatrice (elder daughter of the Duke of York) also have apartments in the palace.

With Levées having been discontinued at the beginning of the Second World War, and with Drawing Rooms and Presentation Parties replaced by Garden Parties at Buckingham Palace, The Queen herself has fewer reasons for coming to St James's, though she does attend a considerable number of receptions in the State Apartments given by charities and other organisations of which she is patron

[88, 89, 90]. The State Apartments are also in frequent use by other members of the Royal Family for receptions, lunches, dinners and concerts, and young men and women who have achieved the Gold Standard in the Duke of Edinburgh's Award are invited to the State Apartments to meet Prince Philip. The only ceremonial occasions held there in recent years were during State Visits by visiting foreign Heads of State, whose programme often included a visit to the palace to receive High Commissioners and Ambassadors accredited to the Court of St James, and addresses of welcome from the Cities of London and Westminster. These ceremonies took place in the Throne Room, which is technically the centre of the Court, and on these occasions

which itself has recently been substantially redecorated [91]; and in 1986 the Picture Gallery was redecorated and re-hung with a rich collection of portraits of the Stuart Royal Family – including several of the mistresses of Charles II [92].

The Chapel Royal underwent a major restoration in 1951–55: the choir stalls were reconstructed, and the Royal Closet redecorated; and in 1980 the organ, which had been presented by King George V, was rebuilt. In the 1951–55 restoration the temporary glass in the north window behind the altar was replaced by Whitefriars tinted glass, and at that time the hope was expressed that 'later a donor might be found willing to present an acceptable stained glass window'. This hope was fulfilled at the time of The Queen's Golden Jubilee, when the 12 great livery companies of the City of London commissioned the design of a new window which depicts a symbolic tree bearing the names of all the Commonwealth countries accredited to the Court of St James, flanked by the four evangelists and surmounted by a dove representing the Holy Spirit, with Windsor Castle in the background. The window was designed by the distinguished watercolourist, John Napper, as his only work in stained glass – but it was completed only after his death in 2001 [93].

The Golden Jubilee work in the Chapel Royal also included the re-ordering of the panelling to provide a new oak reredos behind the altar, designed in the Tudor / Gothic revival style applied earlier by Sir Robert Smirke. The reredos incorporated a triptych of the Adoration by Jan Provoost

the gates in the Clock Tower, always guarded by sentries, were opened so that the visiting Head of State could enter the State Apartments from the colonnade on the west side of Colour Court. In recent years, however, such occasions have been rare because of the curtailment of the programmes for State Visits. Normally those invited to the State Apartments enter by a door in Marlborough Road and pass through the Lower Corridor between Colour Court and Friary Court to the foot of the Grand Staircase.

Apart from the restoration of war damage the palace has changed little since Queen Elizabeth II came to the throne, though there has been a continuing programme of redecoration and a certain amount of internal refurbishment, particularly as residential accommodation has been adapted for office use. In the State Apartments new kitchens were installed in 1968–71, to the west of the Banquet Room,

(1465–1529) which had been purchased by
Charles I, sold during the Commonwealth
and re-purchased by Charles II. At the
same time the pews were re-covered in
purple velvet (inspired by the coverings
in the Royal Pew at Crathie church), the
walls were lined with ashlar as intended
by Smirke, and the 'Holbein' ceiling
was cleaned. Three new panels were
introduced to fill the existing ventilation
panels in the ceiling: one, adjoining the
Royal Closet, shows The Queen's symbol
of the crown surmounted by a lion and
interspersed with heads of corgis; one, over
the nave, shows the emblem of the Duke
of Edinburgh, with dolphins representing
naval service; and the third, near Holbein's
panels depicting feathers for the future
Edward VI, shows the monogram and
feathers of Charles, Prince of Wales [94].

The only other major work during The
Queen's reign has been the reconstruction
of Stable Yard House, at the west end
of the palace opposite Lancaster House
[95]. The stable block erected in 1661 for
James, Duke of York (later James II), and
remodelled by Nicholas Hawksmoor in
1716–17 had fallen into disrepair. In later
years it had been used as a combination
of apartments and offices for the Royal
Household (including the offices of the
Examiners of Plays, who until 1968 carried
out the Lord Chamberlain's responsibility
for reviewing and, if necessary, censoring
plays to be performed at London theatres),
but it had become increasingly dilapidated,
and by the 1950s it was described as almost
unfit for human habitation. Various plans
were mooted for its refurbishment, but
lack of funds – and the imposition in 1965

[93] opposite
The Chapel Royal showing
the Golden Jubilee window.

[94] left
The new Golden Jubilee
panels in the Chapel Royal
ceiling, with emblems of
The Queen, the Duke of
Edinburgh and the Prince
of Wales.

[95] right
Stable Yard House.

[96] opposite
The Queen's Guard
parading in Friary Court.

of a seven-year ban on office building in Central London – meant that nothing was done until the 1970s, when it was virtually rebuilt by the Property Services Agency (successor to the Ministry of Works) with a new raised roof, dormer windows and heavily re-pointed brickwork. The Greater London Council, who had not been consulted about the design, were very unhappy with what the PSA had done, describing it as 'highly inappropriate to the character of a historic royal palace'. However, the building was soon put to good use as accommodation for distinguished visitors attending conferences in Lancaster House, including two of the senior African delegates to the Rhodesia Constitutional Conference of 1979, which led to the independence of Zimbabwe, and senior members of President Ronald Reagan's delegation for the London Economic Summit of 1984. Later it reverted to use by the Royal Household,

and it now houses part of the Royal Collection Department.

In the 1990s the whole of the outside of the palace was re-pointed and repaired over an eight-year period, culminating in the restoration of the Queen's Chapel, where defects in the brickwork were repaired and the hard cement render which covered the brickwork was replaced with lime render; and where lead gutters and rainwater pipes were renewed.

When The Queen came to the throne, there were a substantial number of non-royal residents in the palace: senior members of the Household and some more junior officials who had the right to rent an official residence, and a few retired members of the Household who had 'Grace and Favour' apartments. Now only five members of the Household and a small number of officials, whose duties require them to be resident, are permitted to rent apartments there, and there are no 'Grace and Favour' apartments. The rest of the palace, apart from the State Apartments, is given over to offices. The staff of the Royal Collection, which is responsible for looking after one of the most important private art collections in the world, and which also manages the opening to the public of the royal residences (Buckingham Palace, Clarence House, Windsor Castle and the Palace of Holyroodhouse), have their offices in the palace (and in Stable Yard House). So does the Central Chancery of the Orders of Knighthood (also based in the Stable Yard), which arranges Investitures for those who have received honours in the twice-yearly Honours List, and which looks after the insignia which The Queen presents to them. The Marshal of the Diplomatic Corps, who maintains relations on behalf of The Queen with the Diplomatic Corps and arranges for Heads of Diplomatic Missions to present their credentials to The Queen, has his office in part of York House, appropriately entered from Ambassadors' Court. The Royal Philatelic Collection, the most comprehensive collection of British and Commonwealth postage stamps, is also housed in the palace. The Queen's Guard, who stand on sentry duty outside Buckingham Palace and St James's Palace, have their Officers' Mess and Guardroom in Engine Court, and it is in Friary Court that they parade before the ceremony of the Changing of the Guard at Buckingham Palace [96].

Three of the ancient ceremonial bodies who form members of the Royal Household have their headquarters in the palace. The Gentlemen at Arms, formed by Henry VIII as the Sovereign's Bodyguard, are retired officers of the armed services who parade in their traditional uniforms on State occasions such as the Opening of Parliament and the arrival of State visitors, and two of whom represent the Sovereign at the annual Service held in the Chapel Royal on the Feast of the Epiphany (6 January), when they present the traditional gifts of gold, frankincense and myrrh [97]. Their office in the palace is manned by their 'Axe

[97] top
The Honourable Corps
of Gentlemen at Arms
parading in Friary Court
on their 500th anniversary,
4 June 2009.

[98] above
The Queen's Bodyguard of
the Yeomen of the Guard.

[99] opposite
The Queen's Bargemaster
and Watermen escorting
The Queen on board the
Port of London Authority's
barge, the *Royal Nore*.

based at St James's, and their 'Messenger Sergeant Major', who is in charge of their administrative arrangements, lives in an apartment in the palace. Finally, the Queen's Bargemaster and Watermen, who used to row the Royal Barge when the Sovereign travelled on the Thames, are still on duty in their traditional uniforms when a member of the Royal Family embarks on the Port of London Authority's barge, the *Royal Nore* [99]. They also act as 'boxmen' on the boxes of carriages in royal processions, and on the carriage in which the Imperial State Crown is taken from Buckingham Palace to Westminster for the State Opening of Parliament.

The palace is also home to several of the Prince of Wales's charities, and to the offices of Prince William and Prince Harry. So it is still very much a 'working palace' – more so now than ever, in the sense that most of it is given over to offices. It is a busy place all the year round, so that whereas it is possible to open parts of Buckingham Palace to the public when The Queen is not in residence, this would not be practical at St James's. All that can be seen of the palace are the outside walls – including the remaining Tudor brickwork in the Clock Tower at the foot of St James's Street and in Friary Court in Marlborough Road – and the two chapels, which are open on Sundays for public worship: the Queen's Chapel in summer and the Chapel Royal in winter. For the rest, those who are not lucky enough to be invited inside can only imagine the splendours of the interior and the many colourful events which have taken place over the centuries within these ancient walls.

Keeper and Butler', who looks after the battleaxes which they still carry on formal occasions. The Yeomen of the Guard, an even older corps of royal bodyguards – founded by Henry VII after the Battle of Bosworth in 1485 – are also on duty on State occasions including State banquets, Garter ceremonies, Maundy and Epiphany services and Garden Parties, and they still search the Houses of Parliament on the eve of a State Opening to prevent a repetition of the Gunpowder Plot [98]. They, too, are

MEMBERS OF THE ROYAL FAMILY WHO HAVE LIVED AT ST JAMES'S PALACE, CLARENCE HOUSE AND MARLBOROUGH HOUSE

Henry Fitzroy, Duke of Richmond (1519–1536), son of Henry VIII and Elizabeth Blount, and his wife Lady Mary Howard, daughter of the 3rd Duke of Norfolk

King Edward VI (born 1537, reigned 1547–1553), son of Henry VIII and Jane Seymour

Queen Dowager Catherine (Parr) (1512–1548), widow of Henry VIII

Queen Mary I (born 1516, reigned 1553–1558), daughter of Henry VIII and Catherine of Aragon, married King Philip II of Spain

Queen Elizabeth I (born 1533, reigned 1558–1603), daughter of Henry VIII and Anne Boleyn

Children of King James I and Queen Anne

Prince Henry, Prince of Wales (1594–1612)

King Charles I (born 1600, reigned 1625–1649), and his wife Queen Henrietta Maria

Children of King Charles I and Queen Henrietta Maria

King James II (born 1633, reigned 1685–1688), and his wives Anne Hyde and Mary of Modena

Princess Elizabeth (1635–1650)

Prince Henry, Duke of Gloucester (1640–1660)

Queen Anne (born 1665, reigned 1702–1714), daughter of King James II and Queen Anne, and her husband Prince George of Denmark

Prince William Henry, Duke of Gloucester (1689–1700), son of Queen Anne and Prince George of Denmark

King George I (born 1629, reigned 1714–1727), grandson of Princess Elizabeth (daughter of James I and Anne of Denmark, and of her husband Elector Palatine Frederick)

King George II (born 1683, reigned 1727–1760), son of George I and Sophia Dorothea of Brunswick, and his wife Caroline of Brandenburg

Children of King George II and Queen Caroline

Prince Frederick, Prince of Wales (1707–1751), and his wife Augusta of Saxe-Coburg

Princess Anne (1709–1759), who married Prince William IV of Orange

Princess Amelia (1711–1786)

Princess Caroline (1713–1757)

Prince William Augustus, Duke of Cumberland (1721–1765)

Princess Mary (1723–1772), who married Prince Frederick II of Hesse-Cassel

Princess Louisa (1724–1751), who married King Frederick I of Denmark

Children of King George III (born 1738, reigned 1760–1820), son of Frederick Prince of Wales and Augusta of Saxe-Coburg, and his wife Queen Charlotte

Prince William, Duke of Clarence (born 1765, reigned as King William IV 1830–1837), and his wife Queen Adelaide

Prince Ernest Augustus, Duke of Cumberland and later King of Hanover (1771–1851), and his wife Frederica of Solms-Braunfels

Prince Adolphus, Duke of Cambridge (1774–1850) and (later) his widow, Augusta of Hesse-Cassel

Princess Augusta (1768–1840)

Princess Charlotte (1796–1817), daughter of King George IV and Queen Caroline, and her husband Leopold of Saxe-Coburg (later King Leopold I of the Belgians)

Princess Victoria, Duchess of Kent (1786–1861), formerly Princess of Leiningen, and mother of Queen Victoria

Children of Queen Victoria and Prince Albert of Saxe-Coburg

Prince Albert Edward, Prince of Wales (born 1841, reigned as King Edward VII 1901–1910), and his wife Alexandra of Denmark

Prince Alfred, Duke of Edinburgh (1844–1900), and his wife Grand Duchess Marie of Russia

Prince Arthur, Duke of Connaught (1850–1942), and his wife Louisa of Prussia

Prince George of Cambridge (1819–1904), son of Adolphus, Duke of Cambridge

Children of King Edward VII and Queen Alexandra

Prince Albert Victor, Duke of Clarence and Albany (1864–1892)

Prince George, Prince of Wales (born 1865, reigned as King George V 1910–1936) and his wife Mary of Teck

Children of King George V and Queen Mary

Prince Edward, Prince of Wales (born 1894, succeeded to the throne as King Edward VIII, abdicated and created Duke of Windsor 1936, died 1972)

Princess Mary, Princess Royal (1897–1965), and her husband the Earl of Harewood

Prince Henry, Duke of Gloucester (1900–1974), and his wife Lady Alice Montagu-Douglas-Scott

Prince George, Duke of Kent (1902–1942)

Queen Elizabeth the Queen Mother (1900–2002), widow of King George VI

Children of King George VI and Queen Elizabeth

Princess Elizabeth (born 1926, succeeded to the throne as Queen Elizabeth II 1952) and her husband Prince Philip, Duke of Edinburgh

Princess Margaret (1930–2002)

Children of Prince George, Duke of Kent, and Princess Marina of Greece

Prince Edward, Duke of Kent (born 1935) and his wife Princess Katharine

Princess Alexandra of Kent (born 1936) and her husband the Hon. Sir Angus Ogilvy

Children of Queen Elizabeth II and Prince Philip, Duke of Edinburgh

Prince Charles, Prince of Wales (born 1948), and his wife Camilla, Duchess of Cornwall

Princess Anne, Princess Royal (born 1950), and her husband Vice-Admiral Timothy Laurence

Princess Beatrice (born 1988), daughter of Prince Andrew, Duke of York and Sarah, Duchess of York

SELECT BIBLIOGRAPHY

General

Adair, John: *The Royal Palaces of Britain* (Thames and Hudson, 1981)
Baldwin, David: *The Chapel Royal, Ancient and Modern* (Duckworth, 1990)
Bradley, Simon and Pevsner, Nikolaus: *The Cities of London and Westminster* (Yale University Press, 2003)
Calendar of State Papers (British Library)
Colvin, Howard (ed.): *History of the King's Works* (HMSO, 1963–82), Volumes IV to VI
Glasheen, Joan: *St James's, London* (Phillimore, 1987)
Graeme, Bruce: *The Story of St James's Palace* (Hutchinson, 1929)
Hedley, Olwen: *Royal Palaces* (Murray, 1975)
Pyne, W H: *History of the Royal Residences* (London, 1819)
Sheppard, Edgar: *Memorials of St James's Palace* (Longmans, 1894)
Walford, Edward: *Old and New London* (London, 1897)

Chapter 1

Honeybourne, Marjorie: *The Leper Hospitals of the London Area* (Transactions of the London and Middlesex Archaeological Society, volume XXI)
Rosser, Gervase: *Medieval Westminster, 1200–1540* (Clarendon, 1989)
Stow, John: *Survey of London* (London, 1598)
Sullivan, David: *The Westminster Corridor* (London Historical Publications, 1994)

Chapter 2

Besant, Sir Walter: *London in the Time of the Tudors* (London, 1904)
Chapman, H W: *Edward VI, the last Tudor King* (Bath Chivers, 1982)
Ives, Professor E: *Anne Boleyn* (Basil Blackwell, 1986)
Loades, D M: *The Tudor Court* (London Historical Association, 1989)
Thurley, Simon: *The Royal Palaces of Tudor England* (Yale University Press, 1993)

Chapter 3

Birch, Thomas: *The Life of Henry Prince of Wales* (London, 1760)
Cornwallis, Sir Charles: *An Account of the Baptism, Life, Death and Funeral of the Most Incomparable Prince Frederick Henry, Prince of Wales* (London, 1751)
Grose, Francis: *The Antiquarian Repertory* (London, 1807)
Jesse, J H: *Memoirs of the Court of England during the Reign of the Stuarts* (London, 1857)
Wedgwood, C V: *King Charles I* (London, 1949)

Chapter 4

Burnet, Bishop Gilbert: *History of his own Time* (London, 1818)
Clarke, J S: *Life of James II* (London, 1816)
Curtis, Gila: *Life and Times of Queen Anne* (Weidenfeld and Nicholson, 1972)
Pepys, Samuel: *Diary* (ed. H A Treble, London 1927)

Chapter 5

Beattie, J M: *The English Court in the reign of George I* (Cambridge, 1967)
De Saussure, César: *A Foreign View of England in the Reigns of George I and II* (Murray, 1902)
Hatton, R M: *George I* (Yale University Press, 2001)
McCarthy, Justin: *A History of the Four Georges* (London, 1884)
Plumb, J H: *Sir Robert Walpole* (Allen Lane, 1972)
Sedgwick, R (ed.): *Lord Hervey's Memoirs of the Reign of George II* (Eyre and Spottiswoode, 1931)
Walpole, Horace: *Reminiscences* (Oxford, 1924)

Chapters 6 and 7

Brooke, John: *King George III* (Constable, 1972)
Fulford, Roger: *Royal Dukes* (Penguin, 1933)
Maxwell, Sir H (ed.): *Thomas Creevey Papers* (Murray, 1903)
Russel-Barker and Le Marchant (eds.): *Walpole's Memoirs of the Reign of George III* (London, 1894)
Strachey and Fulford (ed.): *The Greville Memoirs* (Macmillan, 1938)
Sutherland, Duke of: *The Story of Stafford House* (Geoffrey Bles, 1935)
Wilkins, W H: *Mrs Fitzherbert and George IV* (London, 1905)

Chapters 8, 9 and 10

National Archives, Kew
The Royal Archives, Windsor

ACKNOWLEDGEMENTS

I first had the idea of writing this book when I was working in the Royal Household and had the privilege of renting an apartment in St James's Palace. My thanks are due first and foremost to Her Majesty The Queen for granting me that privilege, for her personal interest and encouragement, and for graciously permitting me to use some material from The Royal Archives and a large number of images from the Royal Collection to illustrate the book. I am also most grateful to Her Royal Highness the Princess Royal for writing a Foreword, and to Sir Hugh Roberts, the former Director of the Royal Collection, his successor Jonathan Marsden, Jacky Colliss Harvey, and other members of the Royal Collection staff for their helpful comments on my draft. I have also greatly benefited from information and comments provided by Graham Sharpe, Director of the Property Section at Buckingham Palace and by Jonathan Spencer, Deputy Comptroller of the Lord Chamberlain's Department

Tracking down information about the history of the palace has not always been easy (particularly at four hundred miles distance), and in this I owe an enormous debt to David Baldwin, Sergeant of the Vestry at The Chapel Royal, who has been generous in sharing with me his encyclopaedic knowledge of the subject and whose book *The Chapel Royal: Ancient and Modern* has been one of my principal sources. I have also received much help from Pamela Clark and her colleagues in the Royal Archives at Windsor, Dr Michael Turner at English Heritage, Penny Hatfield (Archivist of Eton College), Stanley Martin (formerly First Assistant Marshal of the Diplomatic Corps) and Colour Sergeant Brian Andrews (Superintendent of the State Apartments) and his assistants. Harvey Van Sickle helped me greatly in navigating my way through the material on the building of the palace in the National Archives, and gave me much valuable advice.

I am also indebted to the staffs of the British Library, the National Library of Scotland, the Guildhall Library and the Library of the University of Edinburgh, all of whom have been unfailingly helpful.

For the illustrations, my greatest debt of gratitude is to Katie Holyoak of the Royal Collection, who has been tireless in responding to my unending requests. I am also grateful to His Royal Highness the Duke of Gloucester, who personally selected for me a photograph of his parents; to Nigel Wilkins of English Heritage; to Sir William Mahon, Standard Bearer of the Gentlemen at Arms; to Clive Stevens, Messenger Sergeant Major of the Yeomen of the Guard, and to Paul Ludwig of Thames River Services.

I have much enjoyed working with working with David Campbell and his team, especially Sandra Pisano, at Scala Publishers who have brought this project to fruition.

Finally, but by no means least, I owe a huge debt of gratitude to my late wife Esme for her help and encouragement, for many invaluable comments and suggestions, and for her meticulous proof-reading. It is to her memory that this book is dedicated.

Kenneth Scott, Edinburgh, 2010

PHOTOGRAPHIC CREDITS